MW01706466

FAT HURTS*

**but change doesn't have to!*

Your Guide to Personal Transformation After Weight Loss Surgery

TIZA PYLE, PhD

Foreword by
James M. Kane, Jr., MD, FACS, FASMBS

YOUR PATH TO SUCCESS COACHING

YourPathtoSuccessCoaching.com

ISBN-13: 978-0-9982289-0-7

DISCLAIMER

This book is designed solely to provide information and support to readers on the subjects addressed. Therefore, the author and publisher disclaim all liability associated with recommendations and guidelines set forth in this book.

This book is sold with the understanding that the author and publisher are not rendering medical, health, or nutrition services. This book is not intended to, nor should it be used, to diagnose or treat any medical condition.

Many of the results achieved by persons cited in this book are not typical for all people, and should not be taken as promise or guarantee of results.

Please consult your personal physician before changing your diet, and/or exercise routine, or taking any nutritional supplements. You should rely on your physician's advice regarding the appropriate choice of strategy for your diet and/or weight loss goals.

References are provided for informational purposes only and do not constitute endorsement of any website or other sources. Readers should be aware that the websites listed in this book as possible additional resources might change at any time.

To my husband, Roger Pyle, who always supports me and gives me unconditional love—no matter what!

And to You, my reader, who has chosen, or is considering, the challenging path of weight loss surgery (WLS) to regain your health and create your own personal transformation. Congratulations on your courage and determination.

Foreword

Imagine losing 140 pounds of your weight…the equivalent of a whole person! Picture yourself standing next to an old friend of many years after that type of transformation, and have them not even recognize you! Impossible, you say? Think again. These examples are everyday occurrences following the modern techniques and procedures used in weight-loss surgery today. This path is not for the faint of heart and, truthfully, bariatric surgery is not the "easy way out."

This transformation can come at a physical, emotional, and spiritual cost that can have profound effects on your personal and professional relationships. I don't suggest that the "cost" will be too high. On the contrary, I suggest that it will be one of the most transforming and self-fulfilling endeavors of your life.

In this book, Dr. Pyle lays out an outline for success following weight-loss surgery. As an expert in the field of "change processes in organizations" for over 30 years, Dr. Pyle guides the reader through the complex transformations that take place from profound physical changes following weight-loss surgery.

Understanding that surgery for weight loss is only one "tool" in achieving overall success of your goal for a healthier and happier life, Dr. Pyle describes the deeper personal changes that are needed for a more long-term, durable weight-loss.

As an expert in the field of bariatric surgery, with more than 30 years of experience, I have had extensive exposure in dealing with patients on this path. I feel this book is a "must read" for coping with the broad changes that will take place in your life.

Success with surgical weight-loss can be a relative goal. An absolute number of pounds shed or the speed at which one loses is different for everyone, and should not be compared patient-to-patient. The overarching goal to success should be looked at in terms of improvement in your medical condition, a reduction in medications, a better sense of wellbeing, ease of ambulation, and a control of habits, which have a direct impact on, and are deeply related to obesity. Surgery for "bad behavior" does not exist. This is a work in progress for personal change. These are attainable goals and this book will help you achieve this.

Concurrently, failure is not an inability to achieve a size 4, have a 34-inch waist, or having some weight regain during your lifetime! Everyone going through bariatric surgery will have some weight regain. THIS IS NOT A FAILURE! Recognizing early these personal habits that bring about weight regain is key to durable weight loss. Attacking these issues with the tools laid out in this book by Dr. Pyle, and having a winning mindset will be a rewarding and lasting remedy.

Finally, undergoing bariatric surgery is a deep personal decision. No one can talk you into this endeavor. If significant weight loss can be achieved with serious diet and exercise, then that is where you should start. However, if you have legitimately tried all other measures with little or no success, weight loss surgery will be a rewarding and effective tool. It can be a "gift" at a second chance. This book will give you the tools to ensure that that gift will last a lifetime.

James M. Kane, Jr., MD, FACS, FASMBS
Kane Center for Surgical Weight Management
Suburban Surgical Care Specialist
Hoffman Estates, Illinois
July 2014

Acknowledgments

My experience with book publishing is that it really "takes a village" to get it done! And it involves a lot of hard work, even when this is your second time around. There are so many steps in the process that the journey can be challenging. I could not have completed this without the help of many!

My heartfelt thanks go to all who have contributed to both the first and second editions of this book. I want to make sure they know how much I appreciate their participation and support in my book-writing journey. This experience has taught me a lot, especially about the generosity of people, and their willingness to support a new author.

Very special thanks go to all who accepted my invitation to be interviewed for this work. Some of you asked to remain anonymous. But you know who you are, and how thankful I am for your willingness to share your stories so others can learn from your wisdom and experiences.

I'm especially grateful to Dr. James M. Kane, Jr. He has supported this project from its start, and graciously agreed to write the foreword. His knowledge and wisdom are evident throughout the book, and greatly valued. Thank you!

A very special "thank you" goes to the editor of the first edition, Gary N. Bowen. His intelligent and judicious input made this book so much better. As an experienced editor and author, he took this "newbie" writer under his wing. Gary was able to ferret out what I really wanted to say and put it in writing for me—or challenge me to do it myself. His contribution is very much appreciated.

The second edition came to life with the support of Heidi Thorne. She kept me accountable and inspired me to stay the course and keep deadlines to complete the work. Thank you so much for your support!

Others who contributed to this process include Alicia Dunams, creator of *Bestseller in a Weekend* program, and her entire staff. I deeply appreciate all the support and inspiration I received from Alicia. Thanks!

Harley M. Storey, Executive Coach, and "The Life Coach Toolman," gave me permission to use some of his material as resources for our readers. The coaching tools, included here as vehicles for further self-analysis and discovery, have added value to the book. I deeply appreciate his generosity in sharing his work and wisdom with me. Thank you!

The mechanics of writing and publishing a book can be daunting. Lenna K. Millar, owner of Audio Transcription Services (ATS) in New Zealand, offered me her expert support to make the first edition a reality. Lenna transcribed the original text, interviews, and completed the initial formatting of the material so it would be ready for the editor's eyes. I owe Lenna a big "thank you" for her contribution to this effort.

I could not have undertaken this project without the support of my dear husband, Roger, and my wonderful friends, who listened to me and offered encouragement to keep going—even when I questioned what I was doing at times.

Many others also provided me with support and friendship during this process. I thank you all!

To all the readers of the first edition who took the time to share their thoughts and suggestions to make the book better, a very special "Thank You!" All your feedback is greatly appreciated, and you started the process of this second edition! I'm very grateful that you cared!

TABLE OF CONTENTS

Introduction

My Reasons for a Second Edition

Since the publication of ***Fat Hurts*** in October of 2014, I have learned a lot, and received valuable feedback on how the book has helped many in their journey to better health. Also, many suggested ways in which the book could be more useful to a larger audience. I really appreciate the feedback I received and thank all for taking the time to engage with me and support this effort.

This second edition incorporates some new information on health and nutrition and offers a revised and enhanced *Section II: Creating Your Future: Your Path of Transformation*.

My personal story of transformation is centered on my experience with weight loss surgery (WLS) and the process of regaining my health through significant weight loss. **However, this book is not about dieting and losing weight. The major focus of my writing is to present ways to develop a positive mindset that allows you to be fully aware of your present and to shift your thinking and feeling to create a new reality.** And as it was suggested by many who read the first edition, this can be helpful to anyone who wants to make changes in their lives, beyond a single focus on reaching a healthy weight.

My wish is that, in this second edition of ***Fat Hurts***, you find helpful information—and inspiration—as you start on your journey of change and transformation.

Why share my story?

Have you ever felt out of place and not very comfortable with yourself? This is how I have felt for a good part of my life, in spite of many successes! And I believe that this experience is shared by many others who are currently overweight, or have something in their lives they want to change.

My story is about my struggles with obesity—or a perception of it! I have dealt with "feeling fat and inadequate" for a good part of my life. And only after having reached a healthier weight, was I able to fully appreciate the price we all have to pay for carrying this extra burden and the impact it has on our health. I want to share my experience with weight loss, and what I have learned from this process of major change, so that others may find the self-motivation to succeed in their quest for a different, healthier and active lifestyle.

Finding this *desired future state* of health and well-being can be accomplished as a result of some change that addresses whatever issue is holding you back. Reaching a weight that is right for you could be an essential first step towards better health and longevity. It is worth the effort.

No one can guarantee that reaching your "ideal" weight will make you happier and solve all your problems. Happiness is something only YOU can achieve. The same challenges you face today will be there tomorrow. But you'll be thinner and healthier. Such hard-won success can't help but give you a different perspective on things, and a better balance in how you solve the challenges in your life. You have chosen to seize an opportunity for better health, more energy and the immense possibilities of an active and productive life as you grow older. But nothing of value is won without daily effort. When we embrace commitment and new ideas, even goals that appeared impossible are within our reach, and self-fulfillment is within our grasp.

What are the two main objectives of this book?

First: This book is being written for you, the person who has felt the pain of feeling inadequate, or "not good enough" due to your weight, and wants to make a change.

I have traveled the difficult path of trying to reach the "right" weight, know its pitfalls, the pain of failure, and the joy that success can bring.

My personal story of weight loss has not been easy, and the journey has been a long one. I have lost more than 50 pounds at various times in my lifetime. The first one was for my high school graduation. Then for my wedding, to get a better job—and the list goes on. Every time I reached my goal. But once the "event" for which I had lost the weight was over, the weight came back. Only, in my sixties, when I decided to do it for myself and for my health—a change in my mindset—was I able to make key behavior modifications that have given me a healthy lifestyle—for life.

Second: You will discover a model of personal change that can support long-term transformation and help you achieve a healthier lifestyle.

In many of the conversations with health care professionals who deal with obesity and its related consequences, it is clear that there is a need not only for information—the WHAT—but, just as importantly, to offer support and tools—the HOW—needed for successful and long-lasting changes.

Any significant transformation in lifestyles and behaviors, in order to achieve a healthy long life, is not an easy process. We are dealing with well-established habits that need to be understood and modified! This is what this book offers: questions to help you find your answers, ideas on how to create your plan to develop new habits, assessments for greater self-awareness, and the opportunity to develop your unique program, based on your needs and preferences.

How to Best Use the Information in this Book

Fat Hurts: Your Guide to Personal Transformation After Weight Loss Surgery is divided into three major sections to better meet your needs.

Each section has a specific focus, so look for the information that interests you. For example, if you already had the surgery, you could skip Section I altogether! The book does not have to be read in order, and the following description of each section will give you more detailed information on what you can expect to find in each chapter of the book.

Section I covers the various methods available to achieve your healthy weight goals for life. Weight Loss Surgery (WLS) is showcased as an important tool to achieve a long-term solution for those who have not been successful with other ways of fighting obesity. It offers a brief description of the various WLS options, and includes a discussion of the key factors in deciding on the most effective program and provider for your surgery. It also provides a brief discussion of possible ways to secure health insurance coverage for the procedure in the United

States.

Section II addresses personal transformation and change. It discusses the importance of creating a vision of your desired future that can guide your journey of transformation. Other topics include a model for the personal change process and the importance of readiness for change. You will find questions to guide your thinking and suggestions on how you can develop your unique personal transformation road map.

Section III suggests a practical plan, using ***"The Holistic Circle of Health: Mindset, Meals and Movement" ™*** as your path to health and productive longevity. It covers the importance of your determination and positive mindset, a brief discussion on the value of various nutrition theories and ways to add movement in your life.

The **Resources** section offers tools and templates you can use to create a plan, track progress and a suggested bibliography to learn more about the process of change and transformation, health, nutrition and wellness.

Having belonged in the "morbidly obese" category based on my body mass index (BMI) for many years, I know the problems—and the pain—associated with this reality. I have been there—where you may be right now!

I am very grateful to have been able to regain my health and energy after losing weight. And this did not happen until some transformation took place within me. I was able to redefine my relationship with food, exercise and to reach my goal of a healthier lifestyle. You may call this the connection of mind, body and spirit. The core of who you really are.

In my journey, I have learned much. Now, I would like

to become your partner in your journey of transformation and good health.

In my website, YourPathtoSuccessCoaching.com, you will find additional information that can further support your journey of transformation and health.

To your continued success!

Peace and Joy,

Tiza Pyle, PhD
Your Path to Success Coaching
www.YourPathToSuccessCoaching

Section I
Embarking on Your Journey: Deciding Your Path

"Once you put your hand on the plow, don't look back, and just keep going!"
Tiza Pyle

This section covers the following key topics:

- Deciding on the best approach for you.
- Learning about the various options open to you.
- Finding the right surgeon and hospital to best meet your needs.
- Understanding the importance of pre- and post-surgery preparation.

There are a variety of options available to address your obesity concerns and they work in different ways for different people. Since this book is primarily about my personal experience with the process of losing and maintaining a healthy weight for life, the emphasis is on Weight Loss Surgery (WLS) and the reasons why it was the best decision for me. **However, this does not mean that WLS is the only way. It's just one of the many choices that are available to you.**

One recurring theme when I talk with "morbidly obese" people is the sense of helplessness that many failed attempts can create. What I have learned is that in order to start your journey to health, sometimes it is necessary to have a fast start. Feeling assured that you can attain quick results can offer the hope needed to continue the process.

This is one of the most important reasons you should select a method that can offer the outcome you wish for. And it's why I chose bariatric surgery as my journey's starting point. Everyone's different.

Deciding on the Best Approach for You

Learning about what works best for you is an important step in finding the solution to conquer your weight challenge. In order to accomplish this and begin developing a picture of how to best reach your goals, answering the questions listed below can be a very good start. You may consider starting a journal to document your thinking about this process!

- How many times in your life have you lost significant weight (more than 20 pounds.)?
- When was the last time you lost significant weight?
- What method(s) did you use? List all the approaches you selected.
- Which approach worked best for you and why?
- How long did it take for you to accomplish your goals?
- For how long did you remain at—or near—your reduced weight?
- What did you do differently to maintain that weight?
- If you regained weight, how much did you regain? And did you gain more than you lost?
- If you regained the weight you lost, what do you think the reasons might have been?
- What are you willing to do differently today to reach and maintain your healthy weight?

There are no right or wrong answers; just helpful information so you can learn more about yourself and what may be the most effective path if—today—you are ready to embark on your journey of transformation to reach your healthy weight for life.

The final decision on the best approach for you is best made jointly with your physician and family. Having a support group to help in your decision can be valuable, as it offers diverse perspectives and shared experiences. That you have chosen to pursue WLS—rather than a more traditional option for weight reduction—is usually a result of many factors, some of which include:

- More traditional approaches that have not worked well in the past.
- Significant health issues that must be addressed to improve quality of life or possible mortality concerns.
- The amount of weight you need to lose to regain your health is significant and needs to be addressed quickly.
- Any risks associated with the surgery are less than those currently present in your clinical case (these are factors that only your physician can properly evaluate).
- You are healthy enough to undertake the surgery and ready to embark on this journey as an option to lose weight —an important consideration that only you can decide.

My Story: Making the Decision

I had lost weight many times in my life; using many different methods. The issue for me was not to LOSE the weight, but to maintain my goal once it was reached. After many failed attempts, it had just become easier to give in and stop trying. But then the extra weight began to seriously affect my health and well-being. My decision to select WLS was based on the following subjective factors:

1. I was healthy enough for this approach. Although some doctors had told me they would not take anyone older than age 60, I checked this information further, and happily discovered that many excellent WLS surgeons do not follow only age, but the overall health of the patient, as the criteria for the surgery.
2. I wanted an approach that would not only help me lose these pounds, but also make it possible to maintain my healthier weight.
3. I was mentally ready for this significant change in my life.
4. I found a first-rate facility and program that met my needs (more on this later).

One important element to consider in making your decision is a clear understanding that **you will be changing your body forever**. You must be prepared for this reality and its significance. For instance: you must accept that you will not be able to eat certain foods because your rearranged digestive system will reject them. It's more than simply deciding not to eat something; it's a matter of accepting that you will no longer be ABLE to eat some foods without causing yourself great discomfort.

I was ready for—and embraced—this approach.

As mentioned earlier, WLS is not the only route to successful weight loss. But it has proven to be highly successful for the morbidly obese, especially those who have tried other ways without sustainable success. You must find what works best for you—in consultation with your physician—and after seeking all the information you can to make this life-altering decision.

Learning about the Various Options Open to YOU

Here, I will share a general overview of the variety of solutions available to you. Much of it comes from my doctor and from the WebMD.com website. But there are many other information resources. And—as mentioned earlier—your doctor is the best resource of all. Being informed enough to ask the most pertinent questions is the biggest help in making the decision that is truly best for you.

What are the Various Types of Weight Loss Surgery (WLS)?

There are two basic forms of weight loss surgery: restrictive surgeries and malabsorptive/restrictive surgeries. Each helps with weight loss in different ways.

- **Restrictive surgeries** work by physically reducing the size of the stomach, which slows digestion. By reducing the size of the stomach to a smaller capacity (2 to 3 ounces of food vs. the normal 3 pints) you eat less and lose weight.
- **Malabsorptive/restrictive surgeries** are more invasive procedures that work by changing how you take in food. In addition to restricting the size of the stomach, these surgeries physically remove or bypass parts of your digestive tract which makes

it harder for your body to absorb calories.

Below is a very brief description of the most common options your doctor might recommend, based on your specific situation.

Adjustable Gastric Banding (AGB). Gastric banding, a restrictive weight loss approach, is one of the least invasive weight loss treatments. This surgery uses an inflatable band to squeeze the stomach into two sections: a smaller upper pouch and a larger lower section. The two sections are still connected; it's that just the channel between them becomes very small, which slows down the emptying of the upper pouch. Gastric banding physically restricts the amount of food you can take in at a meal. Most people can only eat one-half to a cup of food before feeling too full, or sometimes may experience a lethargic or "sick" feeling. The food also must be soft or chewed very well before ingestion.

Sleeve Gastrectomy. This is another form of restrictive weight loss surgery. In this procedure—usually done with a laparoscope—about seventy-five percent (75%) of the stomach is removed. What remains is a narrow tube or "sleeve" connected to the small intestine.

Sometimes, a sleeve gastrectomy is a first step in a sequence of weight loss surgeries. This course of action can be followed-up by Gastric Bypass or Biliopancreatic Diversion when additional weight loss is needed for medical reasons. In the majority of cases, Sleeve Gastrectomy could be the only surgery you need to reach your healthy weight goal.

Gastric Bypass Surgery (Roux-en-Y Gastric

Bypass). Gastric bypass is another common form of weight loss surgery. It combines both restrictive and malabsorptive approaches and can be performed as either a minimally invasive or as open surgery. In this procedure, the surgeon divides the stomach into two parts, sealing off the upper section from the lower. The upper stomach is then directly connected to the small intestine.

The surgeon is essentially creating a shortcut for the food, bypassing a section of the stomach and the small intestine. Skipping these parts of the digestive tract means that fewer calories are absorbed into the body. Unlike adjustable gastric banding, gastric bypass is generally viewed as irreversible, though in rare cases it has been reversed. So, opting for this procedure means that you permanently change how your body digests food.

Researchers have found an encouraging connection between WLS and Type 2 Diabetes. A recent article published in *Science* reports the positive effect of Gastric Bypass surgery on the symptoms of Type 2 Diabetes. As reported by one of the authors of the article, it was found that after the bypass surgery, changes that occur in the intestines cause blood sugar levels to decrease. These new findings are good news that supports the use of this type of surgery!

Biliopancreatic Diversion with Duodenal Switch. This is a more drastic version of a gastric bypass where as much as 70 percent of the stomach is removed, and a larger portion of the small intestine—where nutrients are absorbed—is bypassed. This procedure is also referred to as "the duodenal switch" because it re-routes a portion of your intestine to create two different pathways toward a common channel. Each pathway has a different function in the digestive system and limits the time the body has to absorb calories and fat from the food you eat.

Duodenal switch surgery can also be a back-up option for those who are severely obese and opt for the sleeve gastrectomy described above, but did not lose enough weight with that approach.

Proponents of this WLS option believe that it may be the best way to control high blood pressure, diabetes and obstructive apnea in severely obese people with significant health risks.

Today there is reliable information available on all the possible options and types of WLS. Some of the web-based sources include the Mayo Clinic publications, WebMD.com, and other medical articles that can easily be found by a web search.

Which Weight Loss Surgery Is Best for YOU?

The choice of which procedure is best for you depends on your current health, body type, age, how much weight you need to lose to regain your health, and other key health factors unique to your situation. For instance, if you are very obese, or had abdominal surgery before, minimally invasive surgeries might not be something your surgeon would recommend. It is essential that you discuss all the pros and cons of each procedure with your doctor before making your decision.

Don't be afraid to ask every question that is on your mind until you fully understand the procedure, what it can do for you, the risks and the benefits. It is your life that will change and you should be in control of every aspect of this important decision.

Whenever possible, select a medical center that specializes in weight loss surgery. Studies have shown that the risk of complications is lower when it is performed by experts. No matter where you are, your surgeon must have plenty of experience with your chosen procedure.

Is Weight Loss Surgery Right for Me?

Weight loss surgery is not for everyone. This approach to treat obesity may be recommended for people who:

- Have a **body mass index (BMI) of 40 or more.** This would be about 100 pounds overweight for men or 80 pounds for women.
- Have a lower BMI (of 35 to 40), **but also have a serious health problem related to obesity**, such as heart disease, type 2 diabetes, severe sleep apnea, or high cholesterol.
- Have tried and failed to lose weight by other means.

It is important to be very aware that WLS is one of many options and, when selected as your path to a healthier weight, it will require preparation and the readiness to make significant changes in your life.

My Story: Getting Ready for the Surgery

When I decided to pursue my route of weight loss surgery, I started doing my homework. Research using the Internet was my first step. In 2008, there was much less online information than what is available today. Now, many reliable sources exist to educate you and help you make the best choice for YOU!

In my case, I met the minimum requirements for the surgery listed above: BMI over 40, severe apnea, high cholesterol, family history of heart disease and failure to lose and maintain weight by many other means throughout my life. This situation required attention.

One important concern for me was to follow Medicare requirements for approval of this surgery. In order to qualify for coverage, the procedure had to be performed in a Medicare-approved "center of excellence." This is an important requirement—even if you are covered by other insurance—as it confirms that the hospital you select has met a rigorous approval process and has experience in weight loss surgery.

After many conversations with surgeons, and other physicians, I chose the Roux-en-Y Gastric Bypass procedure. This was based on two key factors: The amount of weight I needed to lose, and my age. I had learned that, at that time, there was more available research on this type of surgery for older patients; the adjustable gastric banding (AGB) was a newer method with less documentation. Also, AGB-induced weight loss would offer less certainty that I would lose the 100+ pounds necessary to ideally benefit my heath. Considering the results many years later—I had my surgery in February of 2009—I'm very happy with my decision. Yes, I need to take vitamins and some supplements for the rest of my life and have committed to yearly blood tests to ensure that I do not have some vitamin and mineral deficiencies that are common side effects for this type of surgery.

Finding the Right Surgeon and Hospital to Best Meet Your Needs

As the popularity and number of bariatric surgeries grow, so do the options you can select. This weight loss surgical procedure is a very personal choice. It is a decision that needs to be made with care, and in consultation with your primary care physician and surgeon. Those with similar WLS experiences can also lend valuable insight into the process. And referrals can be helpful when selecting such surgical professionals.

Below are some questions to consider when making your selection:

1. Do I know anyone who has experienced this surgery and can share information with me about their experience?
2. Who are health care professionals I know (physicians, surgeons, nurses) that can give me information about the various surgical options available?
3. Which hospitals and medical centers in my area offer WLS procedures?
4. Are these facilities properly certified as "centers of excellence" for bariatric surgery?
5. What is the hospital's general reputation?
6. Can I find enough information about the hospital and its physician/surgical group to make an informed decision?
7. How much experience does the surgeon have with my desired procedure?
8. Is the surgeon board-certified in bariatric surgery?

9. Does the medical center/hospital offer pre- and post-WLS programs?
10. Who does my primary care physician recommend as a surgeon?
11. Do I feel comfortable with this surgeon and how he/she answers my questions?
12. Does he/she seem sympathetic to—and respectful of—my needs?
13. Is insurance coverage clear? Does the clinic offer to help me with coverage approval?
14. How does the surgeon's office staff interact with patients and how comfortable do I feel working with them?

This is not an exhaustive list and your questions should not be limited to those suggested above. But this list gives you an idea of the thought you should put in this and why you need to learn as much as you can in order to make **your** most comfortable decision. Asking questions is the only way you will get the information you need to ensure your success with this process.

My Story: Deciding on Where to Go for My Surgery

Once I decided on gastric by-pass as the best option for me, the next step was to locate the surgeon and hospital to perform the procedure. One of my options was the Kane Center for Bariatric Surgery. It came highly recommended as a "center of excellence" for the procedures, which was a requirement of my health insurance program. All the surgeons at the Kane Center are Board Certified in bariatric surgery and have extensive experience in a variety of procedures. The surgical procedures were performed at a well-known local hospital, also accredited as a center of excellence for WLS. There were other options to research, and I did talk with two other surgeons and centers of excellence in the area before making my final decision.

And though I had heard many good things about the Kane Center, what "closed the deal" for me was its pre- and post-surgery requirements. From all I had read, pre-surgery preparation is essential. This is not a decision you make lightly. And your success will depend in great part in knowing what you are signing up for: For life!

In the process I followed, all candidates for surgery were required to participate in a two-hour pre-surgery presentation in order to receive a packet to apply for the surgery. This impressed me greatly. After attending the presentation it became clear that the approach being described by the presenting physician met my needs. This is also the requirement of most bariatric surgery clinics currently, but not as prevalent in 2008. This is a great step in the right direction, ensuring the success of this process for long-term health.

Based on research I conducted to help me make an informed decision, I discovered that most centers of excellence for WLS offer extensive information on their websites. This includes description of various surgery options, their approach, and published articles describing the various procedures. This was an important factor for us—as this was a joint decision with my husband—and helped to determine, and be comfortable with, the surgeon and hospital we selected for my surgery.

The Importance of Pre- and Post-Surgery Preparation

Having a clear understanding of what you need to do before and after WLS is very important and can eliminate problems and surprises as you move through the process.

Some of the key elements of pre-surgery preparation, after you select a surgeon and hospital, involve:

- Insurance coverage.
- Psychological preparation.
- Support from family and friends.

Insurance Coverage. This is an aspect of getting ready for your procedure which needs to be addressed early in the process. And, in a sense, this is one of the easier aspects of pre-surgery preparation. Typically, all surgical clinics have a department that offers support with insurance forms and other compliance assistance to facilitate the approval you need. If this is not available, you might want to reconsider whether you made the best decision on the center that will perform your procedure. Check on this early to avoid problems and delays later!

Psychological Preparation. Change is seldom easy for any of us. When you begin a process that leads to a profound change, such as quickly shedding over 100 pounds, you really are reinventing yourself—for the better. Don't dismiss the impact this change will have in your whole life, including relationships, your work, how you interact with family and friends, along with your own self-image (and awareness).

Another important consideration is to realize that your weight loss is not going to solve all of your life's problems.

Losing weight improves your health and vitality. But you must remain acutely aware of other factors that may have contributed to your obesity. Just losing the weight after surgery will not address any underlining factors or issues. It doesn't solve all of the contributing factors that led to you having all that weight.

For this reason, as has been well documented by research on behavior change, most WLS centers require a thorough psychological evaluation as part of its pre-surgery preparation. This reinforced my belief in the value of receiving some psychological assistance prior to deciding on weight loss surgery in general. As you make the decision to radically change your life, it is essential that you fully understand underlying emotional issues and learn to deal with them. Change NEVER occurs in a vacuum. And all solutions come with their own unique challenges which cannot be ignored or dismissed.

Support from Family and Friends. Some people choose to tell only a few—or no one—about their decision to undergo Weight Loss Surgery. Or they share it with many! It is a very personal decision. However, based on your own personal style, you will need to decide on the type of support that is most helpful.

There is still the misconception that WLS is the "easy way out" of being obese. Be prepared to hear this. But focus on the belief that you have done your homework and—in your case—this "general" perception does not apply to you.

Sometimes we all need to create a protective wall to prevent others' opinions from undermining our decisions. Your research has given you the compelling reasons to pursue WLS. You know it's the right thing for you in the long run. And those who care about you the most—family and close friends—will usually support and reinforce your decision.

In an interview with Dr. James Kane, he shared the following insight concerning the impact of bariatric surgery on relationships:

> *"If you just look at it from the perspective of a marriage, some suggest that 'bariatric surgery makes a bad marriage worse and makes a good marriage better.' So what happens to the personal lives after significant weight loss? With bariatric surgery, the change in the patient is so significant that it does empower people to no longer accept bad circumstances that were tolerated before they started to regain some self-confidence that can be easily eroded when they are obese.*
>
> *Sometimes divorces are attributed to WLS and I'm asked: 'Don't you feel bad? They were married and they broke up after the surgery—one ran off on the other.'*
>
> *However, when you really dig deeper, the majority of the time, a woman (and this happens more with women) tolerated a horrible situation for the majority of her married life. The other spouse understood that he had the reins—the control—over somebody else's life. But with absolute power comes absolute abuse. With WLS, and the profound weight loss, women can find the strength to no longer tolerate these situations, as they regain confidence and self-esteem. They begin to feel good about themselves. And the control they can begin to win back over life can become truly self-fulfilling.*

Similar situations can happen with personal relationships. Some bad relationships or friendships that are built on common misery are jettisoned as well; because the person who has not changed envies the one who is doing something for themselves to improve their situation in life. Eventually that envy becomes palpable for both people; and often, friendships just die on the vine. Other times they end in discord and hurt feelings.

With increased confidence that comes as a result of taking control of one's obesity problem, other changes become apparent: maybe a change in career, or possibly a sudden rise in your position, just because your positive change is noticed. But sometimes, change can cause friends to feel jealous of your success. And often, radical, positive change can tell you who your real friends are.

Jealously and insecurity can be a lethal combination in any relationship, be it professional, friendship or marriage. It makes people do horrible things to each other. I see this often, especially with women. They get thin, and their envious friends walk away because they can't accept their friend has done something so positive when they themselves can't, especially when it comes to obese friends who do nothing to improve themselves. It's jealousy and insecurity on steroids."

So, there may be significant changes in many of your relationships that arise from your decision to take control of your obesity. Sharing your experiences, and having the support of others who are going through the same process, can be very helpful. You become part of a group of people with similar goals and objectives, and who can become the champions—not the detractors—in your journey to better health.

Be prepared for the changes and challenges you will face, and develop the confidence to move ahead with your decision to address your obesity issues. You are worth it!

Section II
Creating Your Future: Your Path of Transformation

Transformation occurs when a vision of a desired future is created and this desire for change is firmly set in your mind. Change is possible! What moves you is the real desire for something different from what you now have.
Tiza Pyle

During my professional life I have been asked whether or not I think a person can change. My unqualified answer is YES and NO!

The YES comes from my belief that we can modify our behaviors, habits and patterns of thinking to become more effective. You have the ability to grow, develop and change to reach your full potential. You can transform your life and reinvent yourself many times to achieve what you want and what is important to you.

And NO! Given my personal experience, and that of my clients, I have observed that your basic personality traits are well established at a very early age. Many of these are hard-wired in our brains and most people are not able to change them. However the following key ingredients for success make change possible:

- Self-awareness.
- A firm desire to develop a different lifestyle.
- Readiness to focus and work at it.
- A clear understanding of the process of change.

In this section we will discuss various aspects of

personal change and how to apply these principles to achieve your personal goals.

The key topics include:

Readiness for Change. The process that is often present when people attempt to make significant changes in their lives.

Stages of Transitions. The key elements of personal change:

- **Developing a Compelling Reason for Change and the Vision of YOUR Desired Future.** The deep motivation for your decision to change, and the blueprint of your transformation.
- **Letting Go of the Past.** Honoring and accepting what has been and being able to move forward.
- **Living (and Acting) in the "In-between" Space.** That uncertain psychological place where the past is no longer acceptable, but you have not reached your desired future state.

The B.A.S.E Model for Personal Transformation. A practical approach to the HOW of real transformation.

You will discover that change management principles are at the core of transformation. There are many change models that provide a deeper understanding of the personal change process. And here, I draw on lessons learned from my experience with change to offer some suggestions on strategies you can use to become more comfortable with the major transformation you are about to experience.

Any change involves discomfort and apprehension. However the pain of not changing has to be greater that the pain of changing. This becomes a very personal choice that only you can make!

My views on change have been greatly influenced by the works of two significant thought leaders: William Bridges and Thomas Kuhn, and for very different reasons.

In the early 1980s, when the initial phases of many major global changes were affecting many corporations and individuals, Bridges introduced the concept of the internal psychological process of change. It was a work that created a revolution in the understanding of what happens to us during those times of external pressures and upheaval in our lives. As he explains, change happens externally; it is something you can observe and is usually perceived by others as well. But when we are faced with almost any type of change, there is another hidden internal process that must take place. It is a journey you must take in order to navigate the external pressures and reach, with some degree of success, this new reality that we both understand and accept. And this happens not only when change is imposed upon us, but also when we initiate change ourselves. This is the micro—very personal—side of the change process.

Conversely, Kuhn, in his book—*The Structure of Scientific Revolutions*—talks about another very important point by discussing large-scale changes that bring significant transformation to the world. He notes that thinking and behaviors shift considerably when there is a significant change that displaces the status quo. And since many people have invested a lifetime working and believing in the "old reality" there is an understandable reaction to the new one. And many people fight to maintain the previously believed reality. Kuhn introduced the concept of *paradigm shift*, to indicate a change that is big enough to transform the world's view of our reality. One example offered by

Kuhn illustrates this point. The change from an earth-centered vision of the universe to the one where the sun is its center. This concept, which was introduced during the Renaissance by Copernicus and later championed by Galileo Galilei, created strong reaction and significant resistance to their views, which their contemporaries refused to consider.

During his trial by the Roman Inquisition in 1616, Galileo was forced to recant his "heliocentric" theory, which placed the sun at the center of the universe. But under his breath he uttered his famous quote, *"All the same it still moves."* This is a wonderful example of somebody who chose to publicly accept the status quo—that the earth was at the center of the universe—in order to survive, but at the same time kept to his belief of a significant change he knew to be true!

It is still not hard to understand why resistance to any new idea remains a strong presence in our lives. When any change is introduced, or suggested, it challenges the beliefs of many people who have invested a lifetime defending the status quo and thus refuse to accept new ideas. There are many examples of such changes in science and philosophy. The lesson is that new ideas and concepts take a long time to emerge, as they challenge the reality that has existed for many years, concepts that are familiar and comfortable to those around you. In short, true change is an evolutionary process, not revolutionary.

Another important concept worth of note is the idea of "readiness for change" and a recognizable cycle in the process of change. The concept was introduced in 1977 by James O. Prochaska and colleagues from the University of Rhode Island.

This model was not without criticism, but it offers an opportunity to better understand change as a process, and to allow for "passage" in each stage, using some useful strategies appropriate for that stage. The authors of the model offer a detailed description and discuss in detail this predictable cycle of change and how it can be used in sustainable behavior modification. An understanding of this process can be of value in your journey of transformation. You will learn not be too hard on yourself, but accept that your reactions to change are normal, and even predictable. Knowing this, and being open to seek support, can accelerate your ability to move ahead in your change process.

When you consider how you have changed, from being overweight or obese to a "normal" size person, it stands to reason that in addition to your personal transformation, there will be another level of change for those around you: your family, friends, co-workers, etc. Your behavior, appearance, and goals, have changed. And from this will emerge a "new you" that others must accept. So be prepared for the ripple effect your new reality will have on others.

In order to successfully navigate this new reality, you can start to use some well-tested principles of change management to support your journey of transformation.

Readiness for Change

"Once you acknowledge that change is not easy, but it is what you want to do, you are halfway there!"
Tiza Pyle

Keeping the above thought in mind, look at the cycle of change model and begin to think where you are in this process, for whatever change you want to make in your life.

Pre-contemplation: Not Ready. Not considering any change. At this stage there is no plan to take any action, and a person can be unware that their present behavior can be problematic. However, others observe the need for change, or may disapprove the status quo. *"Ignorance is bliss."*

Contemplation: Getting Ready. Beginning to recognize that the behavior can be a problem; and ambivalent about any need for change. Weighing up the pros and cons of any action they may take. Not planning any change within the near future. *"Sitting on the fence."*

Preparation: I'm Ready. Starting to think seriously about change, making plans, and starting to take a few steps towards behavior changes. *"Testing the waters."*

Action: I'm Doing It! Putting decisions into clear action and active participation in the process. Acquiring and putting in practice new healthier behaviors. *"In the driver's seat."*

Maintenance: Keep it Going! In this phase, new behaviors replace old. Resolve and commitment to sustain new behavior are the key elements here. In this model, this stage is also transitional, and people need to work towards preventing going back into old habits. *"Cruising along happily."*

Termination: Success! People have developed new ways of coping and are not going back to old habits.

Another important phase that has been added to the original model by researchers and practitioners is **Relapse:** *"Fall off the Wagon."* This is not seen as a stage in itself, but as a return from **Action** or **Maintenance** to an earlier stage. The person can fall back into old patterns of behavior. When this happens, permanent changes in behaviors were not sustained, and the process needs to start again.

An important consideration is to realize that this is not a linear model, and a person can go through the stages many times. Some do not experience **Relapse**. You can stay in the sustained change stage, where new habits are now part of your reality. However, for each new desired change, you may go through the phases of readiness for change.

There is considerable value that can be gained from **Relapse.** This can happen, and if you accept its value, this stage can provide the opportunity to evaluate key triggers and to develop stronger strategies to sustain the desired behavior changes.

Each time a person progresses through these stages of change—and learns from each one of them—relapses become less frequent and have shorter duration.

Understanding the process, and the readiness for change model, can make it easier to accept that new behaviors are not easy to become fully established. What you may be experiencing in your journey of transformation is normal and almost expected! You have the ability to develop new healthier behaviors that will bring you closer to your desired new reality.

Below you will read about "Libby" who was able to change her behavior to deal with alcohol abuse after the surgery. Her story will help illustrate how these various stages in the "circle of change" can be observed. And you will be able to see Libby's progress through the various phases of the readiness model. As you read about her experience, you may also be able to see some of these in your own journey of transformation.

Libby's Story

I met Libby after she had conquered her dependency on alcohol. As we talked, and I learned more about her journey of transformation, it became clear to me that her experience would be of value to many. Knowing about my work on change and personal transformation, she agreed to share her experience, and what she had learned along the way. I thank Libby for this gift in sharing her journey into health. The stages of change will come to life in her story!

Libby is in her 50s and has a demanding career, an active social life and a stable long-term marriage. She has been successful in maintaining her weight loss after gastric by-pass surgery. She has always liked wine, and used to drink regularly, both in social situations, as well as at home. During the preparation for her surgery, she was warned of the changes in her digestive system and the impact these would have in the absorption of alcohol in her system.

"I did not pay much attention to this issue of alcohol absorption in my system and believed I could handle my drinking," she said. *"I have always enjoyed drinking wine and can handle myself."*

Libby is a very engaging and interesting woman. She loves interaction with people, and her active social life gave her many opportunities for "social drinking." And she continued to drink after surgery, not only at parties, but also regularly at home. This was a change from earlier behavior, when food could serve as a great distractor. A couple of glasses of red wine became a bottle—every night. Still, Libby was not able to see any issue with this behavior.

After Libby stopped drinking and talked about this to family and friends, many acknowledged the problem, but also said that she was not ready to hear the truth they were observing. And so, no one said anything, and the problem continued. This is a typical example of what happens in the ***Pre-contemplation Stage*** of change. Others can see the issue, but the person is oblivious of the obvious!

For Libby, the first sign of real trouble started when she could not remember conversations she had had the night before. *"My friends would comment on conversations we had on the phone, or agreements I had made on these calls, and I had no idea I had talked with them. This started to worry me, and it was the first time I started to think about having to do something about my drinking."*

Now we see the start of the ***Contemplation Stage*** in the readiness for change circle. Libby started to acknowledge that she had a real problem and started thinking seriously about solving it. This was a difficult period for her: wanting to do something, but not quite sure of what this may be.

For Libby, ***Contemplation*** lasted for some months. During that time, she even talked with her primary care physician, who dismissed her concerns and reassured her that red wine was positive, and she did not have to worry.

The advice was: *"take it easy and limit the drinking to one glass occasionally."* As Libby relates: *"Good advice, if you can stop at only at a couple of glasses each time!"* Her drinking continued, mostly at home, and very privately. Again, this is not an unusual pattern for many women.

After a few falls in her home at night, blackouts and more worries about the amount of wine she was drinking, Libby started reading about the signs of alcoholism, and recognized many of the symptoms in her behavior. She began to take her problem seriously, and realized that she was an alcoholic and needed real help.

Finding a therapist and naming her problem was the start of the ***Preparation Stage***. Making her concerns public, talking with her husband about needing some help and starting to seek outside help were very positive signs that indicated she was ready to make real changes. However, until a firm, detailed plan for action is done, it is hard to move into the action phase.

Libby still needed a strong reason to help her take the decisive step in resolving the issue. Losing control and verbally abusing her husband in one of her drunken evenings gave her this needed push into real action. For Libby, this was "hitting bottom," a stage in the addictive process recognized as an important turning point in many addiction rehabilitation programs.

Libby was able to move into the ***Action Stage*** when she got some professional help. Her choice to deal with her issue was to stop drinking completely. Once that decision was made, she did not go back in her resolve.

In this stage in her journey of change, Libby completely changed her behavior and had the courage to publicly tell people she was no longer drinking. *"I was surprised by two things when I told people about my decision,*" Libby told me. "*The first was that, for most people, this was a non-event! They really did not care. And the people closer to me were happy that I had made this decision, and were committed to help me stay sober. My drinking had not gone as unnoticed as I had hoped!*"

In the ***Action Stage,*** people change behaviors and these are more visible to others than in any of the previous stages of change. However, as Libby easily recognized in her own journey of transformation, the visibility of the ***Action Stage*** receives most attention and recognition.

This is significant, as having the change you want to make clear and visible helps with accountability. But equally important is to recognize that this is not the only stage in which you can make real progress towards overcoming any issue you want to address.

After more than two years after Libby started her journey of transformation, she continued to be totally sober—in the ***Maintenance Stage***.

It is important to note that Libby's recovery from addiction is not typical. It is a success story, but many have a much harder time in reaching her results!

In a conversation with a therapist who specializes in addictive behaviors, he mentioned that one the biggest barriers to recovery is the inability to move beyond the ***contemplation*** or ***preparation phases*** of the readiness for change cycle. It takes a lot of determination to move into action and stay the course. Understanding and accepting the process of change is a great step in the road to recovery. In Libby's case, after identifying her problem, she was ashamed and felt quite lost, but she did not deny the issue. Denial of a problem can greatly delay its resolution.

Among the many possible consequences of post-gastric by-pass surgery—many belonging in the life-saving category, while others not so positive—alcohol addiction, or other types of compulsive behaviors can be a real issue.

Libby's situation is not unique, and addictive behaviors have to be considered, and addressed, in the journey of recovery after surgery. A possible cause of obesity is food dependency, and these tendencies do not magically disappear with the surgery!

Not all people who have WLS become addicts, but it appears that many have to consider the issue of dependency in their lives once food is no longer an option. And for many, when this issue is not addressed, weight gain after the surgery can also happen.

In this next section, another important aspect of change is discussed to help you use some great tools to support your healing journey.

Stages of Transitions

"Just when the caterpillar thought the world was ending, she turned into a butterfly."
Proverb

Another helpful tool you can use in your journey is an understanding of the normal stages of personal changes—transitions—that can be expected when human beings experience any type of change. And these can be both positive and negative changes you may experience in your life.

The major components of any personal change include:

- Creating a Vision of your Desired Future
- Developing a Compelling Reason for Change
- Letting Go of the Past
- Living in the In-Between Space

Creating Your Vision: Declaring Your Dream

"Knowing where you want to go is the key to your success. Without this clear vision, any path will lead you nowhere."
Tiza Pyle

Below are a few ideas on how to develop your vison for the future you want. This can become the story of what you want to be and do with your life, and you have a chance to make it bold and wonderful. Look into your heart and think big!

These questions are "thought starters" that can help you to develop your vision:

- What is your dream for your life?
- What you would like to change or do differently?
- What you would like to keep and take forward into your new future life?
- What would your success look like once you achieve what you want/dream?
- What would you be doing, thinking, and how would your behavior change in this new life you designed?

Write down what you decide and make your vision as detailed as you can. Learn to visualize yourself in this new state of being, in detail and vivid color!

As you embark in this metamorphosis, knowing how you want your new future to be will be a great asset. If you are morbidly obese, and are working toward reaching a healthy weight for yourself, changes in your life while you are working towards your goal—and after you reach it—will be significant.

Being able to visualize your desired future and what you want to accomplish once you attain your normal weight and your healthier, more active lifestyle—or any change you want to make—gives you the needed motivation to stay the course. This is the first step in any change management process: ***your desire for something different from what you now have.***

The clear vision of the desired future, followed closely by your strong desire for making a change—your compelling reason—will help you get there. In the corporate world there is a common phrase: "the burning platform." Nobody wants to jump into a freezing North Atlantic sea. But if your oil platform is on fire, you must jump if you want to survive! The same is true for personal transformation. You need a compelling reason to change!

Deciding to use of a journal to record your thoughts could be very helpful. This may not be easy for many, including me! However, writing down what is in my mind helps me with letting things go and being able to move on. It also provides clarity and focus. It is a very freeing experience!

Linda's Story: Success Without WLS

Linda's account of her change is a great example of someone who was successful in her weight loss journey through non-surgical means. She chose the *Take Shape for Life* program, a meal replacement approach that helps clients reach their healthy weight quickly, using the support of a health coach to create behavioral changes for long-term success.

One of my previously mentioned objectives is to show that WLS is not the only method for you to achieve a healthier weight for life. However, various stories tell us that there is a common thread of motivation, structure, discipline and support that makes this important and positive transformation possible.

Linda reached her healthy weight in 2010, losing a total of 80 pounds. She has maintained it since. Linda is now a health coach for the *Take Shape for Life* program. Here is her story of success:

> *"What worked best was to have a structure that was healthy for me. This was a very important point in selecting a way to reach my weight loss goals.*
>
> *When I set my mind to something, establish goals and believe in them, I take a step-by-step approach to achieve the results that I want. So the highly structured approach of this program worked best. As I began to see and feel results, it was not only inspiring, but reinforced my structured approach. And as my weight loss progressed, I felt even better about myself. As I approached my goals, I began applying my structured approach to developing weight maintenance habits because I never wanted to go back to where I had started."*

When we explored the potential difficulties in her journey to a healthier weight, Linda offered this insight:

> *"The biggest struggle was changing my behavior when eating out. I got to the point of saying to my family, 'You decide where you want to eat and I'll figure it out.' Then, I would pour my thoughts into staying with my weight loss program without intruding on the rest of my family's*

dining experience—or at least as little as I could. I would ask the waiter if it was possible for the chef to prepare my meal in a way that allowed me to continue my journey. To my surprise and delight, I was almost universally accommodated with barely a complaint or resistance. All I had to do was ask nicely."

In explaining her weight loss approach Linda offered this thought:

"Medifast (a meal replacement formula) is used initially to lose weight. But you are not eating this for the rest of your life. It's a temporary, healthy piece—albeit a small part—of a healthy journey. And you're eating much smaller portions six times a day.

One of the meals in my program included lots of healthy greens and protein. I've learned more about my body and how my body processes foods as I lost weight than I ever did in any other program. I learned it's beyond just eating the food. It's about understanding the nutrition of the food that you're eating and how your body naturally functions on a daily basis by eating every two to three hours. As I'm fond of telling my clients, it's giving your body premium fuel and everything it needs to recreate a very happy body."

Another important element of Linda's current coaching practice is to help people maintain their new weight after reaching their goals. She offers the following advice, based on her own experience and the work with clients:

"Stay focused on what you want."

"Know that is about making conscious choices to stay healthy. Every day I know I have choices to make: how I move my body and what I eat. You have to think about it every day. It's a lifestyle change based on self-awareness and commitment."

"Be active: Daily activity is essential. As people begin to lose weight, exercise becomes easier. In my own experience—and this may sound very silly—I literally felt lighter on my feet when I wore tennis shoes. I felt like I was walking on a cloud. And every day I found I could move a little better and a little farther!"

Linda's own success, and her commitment to support others in their journeys, shows that there are many different paths you can take to live healthier.

Developing a Compelling Reason for Change

If you do not find a powerful reason to sustain you in the journey of change, success may become elusive.
Tiza Pyle

The first step in your personal transformation process is a clear picture of your *desired future*. Call it vision, desired future state, or whatever makes sense for you. It is the destination of your transformational journey and must have a meaning for you. Transformational processes apply to organizational, as well as personal change, but with one major difference. Personal change is essentially private and happens inside of you first, before others can see your new reality.

When applied to the process of changing from being an overweight or obese person to a "normal" size person, you must understand what you have to let go of in order to achieve your desired state and develop a better understanding of how you have benefited from being fat. Yes, you read that correctly. I did say *benefited*!

As you start your journey into a healthier lifestyle, I invite you to answer the following questions of yourself—honestly. Using a notebook or journal to record your thinking about this process can be very helpful and give you an opportunity to gauge your progress.

- What is the most important reason for me to make significant changes in my life to reach my ideal weight?
- How has being fat benefited me? Write down two or three reasons where being overweight or obese

helped you. I am sure you will find a few!

- What has changed in my life now that I have found the strength to address my weight issues?

Having a compelling reason for your transformation process is a key element of success. In many cases, a significant health risk was the main motivator for the change. Below are examples of reasons that have moved three women to start the process of transforming their lives to regain their health.

Kay's Story: Accepting the Need to Change to Improve Her Health

Kay was in her late fifties when I met her. She was able to regain her health and self-confidence after accepting that her obesity threatened her ability to live a long and healthy life. When I last talked with her, Kay had lost 64 pounds (29 kilos) in 16 months, and regained confidence and self-respect while conquering her obesity.

> *"After I was diagnosed with Type 2 Diabetes, I was shocked and realized that if I did not do something about my obesity I could probably die. So, my main goal and method was the most painstaking thing I've ever done. I started going to a park not far from my house, just up on a hill and kind of private. I began slowly walking around a running track. It's a large one. I found it hard to just walk, but forced myself to do this every day—one day at a time—a little farther each day. I was so hugely overweight and also had asthma that made it difficult to even walk up my driveway without feeling physically distressed, to the point of occasionally needing medication.*

My other challenge was to shift my mindset to **want** *to change my life by losing weight. Every morning I had to force myself to go out for those walks. It was a chore I didn't want to do. But every day I forced myself to take those walks in that park and felt a little bit better. And that made it a bit easier to take the next walk the next day, and the next day, and the next..."*

Abby's Story: Addressing a Serious Health Issue

As a young woman with small children, and a successful chef before she became seriously ill, Abby had to make many adjustments in her life. Her medical condition created stress and immobility that made her less able to cope with her obesity. In her late 30s, she could carry the extra weight. But later, as she confronted her serious new health challenges, obesity caused her further problems and made her much less capable of leading a productive life. She describes what was happening to her.

"I couldn't even walk up a flight of stairs. I absolutely HAD to do something in order to be healthier and more mobile for my young boys. I don't think any of it (the surgery) should be taken lightly. It's a serious life commitment. The decision was hard. It took months for me to decide whether I was going to do this. I—along with my husband—decided it was something we would need to accept. But we also knew it would be a life-altering decision. What helped with my decision was that I wanted to be healthier for my family and for myself, to be able to play with my kids again rather than be in bed or a 'couch potato' during the day."

Karen's Story: Finding a Lasting Solution to Improve Her Health

Karen was in her early 40s when she had her weight loss surgery in 2009. Since then, she has lost over 200 pounds. She tells her story:

> *"I was seriously obese, with a BMI of over 60. A BMI between 19 and 24 is considered normal. I had tried many diets over the years and none worked for me. I needed help. At the time, my triplets were nine years old.*
>
> *I had yo-yo dieted since I was a teenager. But all I ever ended up with was more weight. I knew the right foods—and portions—to eat. I understood dieting. But every time I began one, I couldn't stay on it. Traditional dieting wasn't working and it was only getting worse. As my health continued to deteriorate, I knew I needed external help and I finally buckled down and admitted that what I needed was some type of Weight Loss Surgery.*
>
> *I did my homework and chose the AGB as the best solution for me. After some research I was able to locate a surgeon who had a lot of experience with this procedure who holds many patents on some of the laparoscopic tools used to insert the LAP-BAND® System. The device is typically used for those who need to lose less weight than me. However—because of my situation and my determination—the surgeon believed the AGB would be successful."*

In addition to finding a compelling reason for your change, and developing a clear vision of your desired future, you will discover more options for moving ahead with your transformation process when you develop a good understanding of what you need to let go of in order to move forward. Until you tackle this "letting go process" there is a danger of allowing the past to hold you back, preventing you from reaching your goals and the future you want.

The past is an integral part of who you are. But it cannot become an anchor that holds you back. You must let go if you want to move forward.

Letting Go of the Past

"Remember what was with love and kindness, and then let it go, so you can learn to live in the present"
Tiza Pyle

Creating a new reality means that something about your current life must change, and you must enter unfamiliar territory, something that you do not know or have not experienced. Your present may be painful. But it is known. And there is a strong measure of comfort in familiarity. But to grow and change, you must take the risk of letting go of what you know and objectively examine the actions, behaviors and beliefs that are creating your current reality.

As you prepare to let go of the past, there is also the feeling that if you decide to move forward, your past must be denied. This is untrue and is something very important to realize in the process of personal change.

Personal transformation asks you to understand and respect who you are and what you have done, without assigning blame or "right and wrong" for your present or past reality.

Every change requires letting go of something and sometimes includes a mourning period over what is about to end—just because you are giving up something that is familiar. Hanging on to a past you want to change delays your journey and robs you of the energy you need to make your transformation. Following are some questions you might want to ask yourself to support a transition to your desired future:

- What might be preventing me from moving ahead and changing my current reality?
- What do I now have that can support me in making the changes I want to make in my life?
- What are two or three important lessons I have learned from my past that can help and support me in the future?

When you apply these principles of "letting go" of obesity, you may ask yourself, "*Why do I hang on to something that is not good for me, or has caused me pain?"* As hard as it may be to understand, there are benefits to being obese. You have experienced these benefits, sometimes to the point where they support your current reality. As you embark in your transformation, try to understand how your present life has helped you. It can give you insights on how your entire system of living may need change. This could include long-ago learned behaviors, beliefs, habits, and even relationships that are now part of your life, might deserve serious review.

Do not be afraid to "be afraid." Fear is healthy because it makes us cautious. No change is easy. And though you are not fearless, you can control your fears. The decision to reshape your life—and yourself—has both risks and rewards. Believing in yourself and the possibilities that lie ahead of you will provide the strength you need to move into your desired future.

Critical Thresholds on the Journey of Self-Transformation

We all experience important times in our lives when we know our next stage will bring significant changes in ourselves and on our way of "be-ing." And such times involve many types of changes.

As you prepare to let go of the past, consider these times of change as *"critical thresholds"* in our life—times when you start a new way of being or becoming. To help you better identify these times of opportunity, below are a few characteristics of critical thresholds that can open the possibilities for profound transformation.

A threshold marks the start of a new way of thinking, and behaving, of "being and becoming."

The principal function of a threshold is to bring awareness of the need to move beyond the present, into a new mode of being and behaving.

As a threshold appears in your journey you have a choice of stepping over it and moving on, or stop and stay where you are. It a choice you can make!

The qualities of critical thresholds are being *radical* (you will not be the same), *irreversible* (you move past your present reality) and *successive* (once transformation starts, it has the power to sustain changes).

A critical threshold affects your roots, attitudes, values and convictions. These are challenged into your journey into a new reality.

These changes are not orderly and always progressive. Your transformation journey will continue forward, as you move towards a new stage of your life.

Change and personal transformation are not easy, but the rewards can be significant. You can chart your future and become a true owner of your life.

Abby's Story: Letting Go of the Past

Abby is a good example of the importance of needing to "let go of the past" and learn to live a new life for herself and her family. She had to create a different vision for her future—complicated by serious health issues. Conquering her obesity problem was an important element of regaining health in many fronts. Now her vision of the future is clear and Abby knows what she wants to achieve. But she is still trying to make sense of what is happening to her along the way.

At her highest weight, Abby's "40 BMI" classified her as morbidly obese, with corresponding serious health consequences. She had also been diagnosed with unspecified Crohn's disease (a form of inflammatory bowel disease). The accompanying pain of this illness further aggravated her condition and amplified her daily difficulties. After consulting a team of physicians, it became clear that surgical intervention was the best option to deal with her illness. Although the bowel resection surgery that was performed to relieve the symptoms of Crohn's disease, it is not one commonly used in bariatric surgery. Abby anticipated that she would lose a considerable amount of weight throughout the course of her treatment. She needed to be prepared for this significant change.

Another issue that affects Abby in this stage of her transition is how she deals with changes in her social life. This has caused some post-surgery anxiety and well illustrates the need to "let go" of the past in order to move into a new healthier reality.

Here is how Abby describes some significant changes when she now gathers with family and friends:

"A massive change was our socialization, and how we got together with friends and family. My friends know I don't

eat out anymore because it challenges my will-power. I'm in the restaurant business, so going out was very much part of our family routine. The same holds true for my "kitchen experiments" as a chef, and wanting to prepare these elaborate meals every time family and friends came over. My life revolved around food, and I needed to make significant changes to shift the focus from just food and being in the kitchen.

It is sad that we don't entertain nearly as much as we did. But the behavior modification is reinforced every time I look in the mirror or revel in how delighted my family is with the 'new me.' And that's what counts most."

Abby also sees many positives arising as a result of this shift in focus away from food in her relationship with family and friends as she reshapes her future.

"One very interesting change is that I'm finally learning to enjoy the company of family and friends. My kitchen used to be my retreat. And my role in both our families was to be this 'experimental scientist' concocting new dishes, while the rest socialized in other rooms. Today, I'm not in the kitchen nearly as much as I used to be. I'm a part of the conversation. I'm learning more about these people, their likes and dislikes, who they really are. And it's fun.

I'm still growing comfortable with this profound change in how I relate to others. But in doing so, and gauging the results so far, I understand why you have to give up familiar habits if you want to realize new—and better—dividends in life."

In this process of personal transformation, Abby is learning how to modify old behaviors and create experiences that can support her new life and the choices that she has made. This process takes time and involves understanding that you will need to accept when letting go of your past. Appreciating the discomfort and uncertainties of the "in between" stage of your transition is an integral part of creating a new future.

Living in the "In-Between" Space

"Welcome the unknown! Within uncertainty lies all possibilities!"
Tiza Pyle

Perhaps the most challenging time in any personal transformation is learning how to accept and be comfortable in the difficult "in between" spaces of your metamorphosis: when all the changes start to happen.

You're not the person you were, but not yet what you want to be—and do. This is an integral stage of all personal change, with much confusion and uncertainty. But it is also exciting, once you understand how to best take advantage of new possibilities. You can create your future and be who you really want to be, doing what you want to do. But it takes time, effort, and a commitment to move—sometimes relentlessly, and not always swiftly—through this phase of your transition.

Developing a support network is a key to your success. We've already explored how bariatric surgery's likely impact on relationships cannot be ignored. Other profound changes can occur as you lose weight and develop a different approach to your life. You will need to observe the reactions of others as you change and make sure you find people who can offer the support you need. The impact on family and friends can be significant, which is why it is really important to consider their responses to your transformational journey.

Your family and friends need to know and accept that you're becoming a different person. And many—by habit—might resist your change, which is to be expected.

So all of a sudden when you unexpectedly say to your kids, *"I'm going to go to the gym guys, do your own laundry,"* can surprise or even shock them. It is important to accept that your effort at self-care is not being selfish, as some might think. It merely shows that your priorities are changing; and you are not the only one who will benefit. Your family and friends want you to be healthy and live longer, right? If creating a new lifestyle supports your goals, in the end, all stand to benefit. That's not to say these changes won't create tension among family and friends along the way, or at least puzzle them. This is why you must work to make others understand—even if only by your behavior—that there's something in it for them too. Some might even make you feel guilty of your "misplaced" agenda. So be careful not to slip back into old habits of, *"Oh, my kid or my spouse needs me more."* And don't confuse misplaced guilt for need, especially if you're being quietly pressured into NOT doing what is important to you by those who know how to push your "guilt buttons." Keep strong and focused. Both are vital in modifying your new, healthy thoughts and habits.

This "in-between" space is a great opportunity to identify your personal needs and then act on them. Taking steps to identify where actions are centered seems harder for women than men. But it's something you must do for your own self-improvement. Social pressures and expectations tend to place women in roles of subservience, which makes it easier to forget that we must serve ourselves first—before we can conscientiously serve others.

The importance of learning how to attend to your own

needs was made very clear to me during one of my many air travels. When I REALLY HEARD what the flight attendant was saying: ***"put your mask on first before helping others,"*** it was clear that self-care is not a selfish act. Self-preservation is essential to successfully reach our life's purpose, even when that purpose is service to others.

I had to learn how to be clear about what I needed and wanted. Many do not know how to do that, which can sap well-meaning energy to the point where no one benefits. I strongly believe such attitudes cause overeating in some. When one's reality starts to change, others can strive to keep the "status quo," which in this case, ends up being at your spiritual expense. As you learn to recognize how relationships are impacted by your transformation, you'll likely learn to better deal with such potential "distractions of spirit" and discover how to stay your course.

Friends' responses to your "new way of doing things" can be very compelling, especially those which may be associated with your obesity. For example, a person I met in a bariatric surgery support group— "Mary"— was the fat girl who went to parties and was expected to stay at the table and take care of the purses and coats, while everybody else danced and had fun. She was rarely invited to dance because of the way she looked, and behaved—shy and lacking confidence.

But as the weight began coming off and her beauty grew more apparent, she became more self-assured and realized the "slot" her circle of "friends" had subconsciously placed her in. It didn't take very long until she told them, *"I'm not sitting here taking care of purses any more guys. Take care of your own stuff."* As you can guess, due to Mary's "assumed" role as the "fat girl," some were taken aback when her "rebellion" caught them off-guard.

Other examples of relationships that are predicated on being fat are situations where food is the primary reason for gathering. As you no longer accept the same type of foods that made you obese, these friends may resent you. Or you may decide that a certain group no longer offers the support you need to embrace and maintain your new lifestyle. Most relationships are transitional, some just have longer evolutionary periods than others. Those based on circumstance are often casualties. As your situation changes, you may be compelled to reevaluate some of these friendships. Those relationships that stand the test of time—and the challenges of change—are the ones with people who accept you for you; and not with those with whom you shared what turned out to be shifting common interests.

Learning to develop new habits and different routines for a healthier life are the major challenges experienced during transitional periods we all must go through. And this series of experiences is more than just losing weight. It's also about understanding how the changes you are experiencing become catalysts for new roles and a lifestyle you may not have experienced before. Significant weight loss (or any other major change in your life) can serve as a bridge to a great new way of understanding and assessing your current relationships in new and better ways. Embrace this growth as a gift and use it to your advantage.

Below are seven questions that—once answered honestly—can give you helpful insights for success during this "in between" space of your personal transformational journey:

- What are two or three habits I want to change in

order to be successful in my desired new life?

- What must I do differently to change the above habits?
- How will these changes impact my life? How will I be different?
- How will I know I am reaching my goals? List two ways to measure progress at making these desired changes.
- What consequences might I suffer if I do not make these necessary changes? How can I prevent this?
- Who might be negatively impacted (and how) by these positive changes in me?
- Who can help me to reach my goals? List the names of at least three people who can offer the support to make these changes.

All true change takes effort and commitment. Personal transformations are very rewarding and hard to achieve without strong resolve. Motivation is something that only you can find. But once it is found, that inspiration is a key element in your success.

Kay's Story: The Importance of Support

Learning to ask for—and receive—support from others was another success factor for Kay as she operated in the "in between space" of her transformational journey. In addition to finding a mentor to support her, Kay opened her world to other important relationships in her life.

"Until my self-confidence grew, I had isolated myself from the world. But along with the weight loss came a newfound ability to open myself to others.

For years, I was accustomed to doing things on my own with the false belief that 'I had to do it myself.' But I couldn't. However, when my world started to open up due to the increase in my energy level, I was less afraid of going out in public. I began to rediscover myself. I had started my business out of my home in 2009. And I was able to pour a lot of that reinvigorated energy into this new enterprise, which also began to grow with my self-confidence. I began allowing more people into my world. My weight loss has changed my life for the better on so many fronts: emotionally and socially. Another welcome change was really inviting my daughter-in-law into my life."

Kay reinforces some key points made earlier, that are common to many people going through the experience of redefining their lives.

- Find someone who can—and is willing to—support you: a doctor, a mentor or a friend. Somebody who cares and can get you to take those difficult first steps.
- Allow people to support you through the process even though you would prefer that they do not. You could discover why you really **can't** do it on your own.

- Reach out to others and allow them into your life. It's one of the most important lessons we can apply, ever!

The Changing B.A.S.E. Model ™

A Practical Application

I have always believed in finding out HOW to do things, not only what to do and why. As mentioned before, I lost the majority of my extra weight in 2009, during the first year after the surgery. And since then, have also been able to lower my weight to healthier levels. I am very grateful for being able to achieve such results after the WLS surgery, but it has not been without some challenges!

So, one question I have asked myself is: "*What have I done to make this happen?*" From this reflection and personal exploration, the ***Changing B.A.S.E. Model*** was born. This is a very practical 4-step process that can be used during many types of changes.

- **B. Believe** that change is possible and you have the ability to discover and reach your potential. You can do something different to accomplish what you want.
- **A. Acknowledge/Accept** who you are. This is the basis for what you may want to become. Develop a strong sense of self awareness and accept the need for change. It is not easy, but YOU can do it.
- **S. Seek** support to ensure the success of the change (people and processes). Look for real help in your journey.
- **E. Execute** a plan that is, first, customized to you and meets your needs and, second, is a sustainable way to guide you in your journey.

This is a simple, but powerful, model—the practical **How-To**—that can allow you to write your own story and re-invent yourself as many times as you want. The goal is to become YOUR best in each stage of your life.

I have used the ***B.A.S.E.*** approach many times in my life, in an instinctive way, and without being fully aware that this really represented an organized process that could be repeated many times with very positive outcomes. Only recently this process was consolidated in my mind as a structured model that I wanted to share with others. You can use this model as the foundation for success in your own personal transformation plan.

In order to make this approach more real for you, I have described below my own journey of change and how I used the model to reach a lower weight to help control sleep apnea.

During my obese years, I was diagnosed with severe apnea, and was using the CPAP (continuous positive airway pressure) machine to help me sleep better and to reduce the impact of apnea in my life and health. It was not easy—or comfortable—and my compliance rate was not very high!

As my weight reached more normal levels, the symptoms of apnea improved and after a check-up, my situation was considered "borderline." That was when the physician said something that really was exciting to hear: *"Lose about 10 more pounds and you may not need the machine."* This was good news. However, to lose 10 additional pounds—and maintain the lower weight—was not an easy task! Remembering how I make changes in my life, I started working with my Changing ***B.A.S.E.*** Model! This time, I decided to do this in a more purposeful way, paying attention to the different steps I need to follow.

Believe you can do it. For me, the key motivation that

supported a mindset shift was my desire to be free of the CPAP machine and to trust that losing the weight would do the trick. Remember that I was already at a very comfortable weight for me and had developed a way of eating to maintain it. This would have to change!

Accept that change is necessary and it can be hard. Another important step for me! Over the years, I have worked at self-awareness and I know well how I can sabotage my best efforts by negative self-talk and lack of trust in my ability to let go and make changes. Until you fully accept what has to change and recognize that what you are doing currently may not work, real and sustainable change may not happen. This step in the model is essential and it takes hard work!

Seek support. I really like the thought: *"You have to do it (the change) yourself, but it does not have to be* ***by*** *yourself."*

Find people who can support you in this process. For me, one important aspect of finding help was to identify a friend who could become my accountability partner. I needed someone who would help me stay on track. My husband was another important partner is this process, as I was going to change how we eat!

Execute the Plan. This last step is the tactical portion of the model. You already know WHY you want to make the change, WHO you can enlist to support in the process, and now you need the HOW.

My plan to reach the new ideal weight for me had four parts:

1. *Write down what I eat.* I have learned over the years to use this only as a "data point" from which I can learn about how my body responds to food. I know well how hard this can be, as it carries the

judgmental thinking of "being good and being bad." When I ate ice cream or cookies, I would record this on my food diary. I really learned how to use this information only as data to help me better manage the process. There are many excellent web sites and apps for your various electronic devices that you can use to help you with this step.

2. *Develop a practical food plan.* I had to decide on the best approach for me and what foods I was going to eat. There are so many "perfect" diets, that it is not hard to get confused by information overload! In my opinion, the key is to choose something that works for you and your body type. For me, based on what I know about my own metabolism, in order to lose weight I need to focus on a high protein/low carb approach. This includes all types of meats, cheese and carbohydrates, primarily from vegetables and some fruits. And I need to avoid refined sugars and processed grains. For you it may something different, but in my experiences, you will need a plan to be successful. And going back to the first step in the model, believe you will reach your goal of a healthier weight.
3. *Stock the kitchen with the foods I will need.* This was an important step for my success. Having what I wanted to eat readily available in the house makes the process easier and less stressful. My suggestion is to prepare menus for the week (to help with the shopping) and have fun planning and preparing exciting food.
4. *Commit to an exercise routine.* Moving your body is

essential and, for me, it was necessary to schedule exercise in my day as an important commitment. And to this day, this is not easy for me, but necessary to maintain my healthy weight. Exercise has to become an important priority for life!

The approach described above helped me achieve a new weight level and to be able to stop using the CPAP machine. To maintain my change, I have to work at it daily, but it is worth it for me. I wish the same for you, in the changes you decide to make!

The ***Changing B.A.S.E. Model*** is simple, and it works! However, change is always hard, so its application to a real situation can be challenging.

Believing that you can do something new and different is not easy and, in my opinion, the hardest part of this model. So much gets into the way of creating a clear intention of what you want to achieve. Old habits, beliefs, and assumptions have a way of creating barriers that prevent you from moving ahead to BE and DO what really matters to you. But you have the power to make the changes that matter to you in your life and create the future you want.

Section III
Making it Happen: The Holistic Circle of Health™

Without a strong desire for the new—a change in mindset—no diet and exercise will create the new reality you want.
Tiza Pyle

Developing a Structure to Support your New Life

The previous section, *Creating your Future: Your Path to Personal Transformation*, provided you with the framework for personal change.

The *Holistic Circle of Health* model allows you to develop a structure to support your new life. It includes three key elements—**The 3 Ms**:

- **Mindset:** Your readiness to accept change.
- **Meals:** Your choice of the food you eat.
- **Movement:** The types of exercise you select to best meet your needs.

This may seem very simple, but working the model is not easy. Success is attained only when the three elements are holistically integrated into your life. And though all three elements are necessary, the change in mindset is the primary driver of long-lasting success. Until this is understood and integrated into your plan, long-term sustainable change cannot happen.

This Section offers practical suggestions and tools to help develop your plan for long lasting changes and success in your journey to better health and longevity. This is the "how to" part of this book:

- Creating a Winning Mindset.
- Choosing the Right Meals for Your Needs.
- Making Movement Part of Your Life.

Creating a Winning Mindset

"The mind is everything.
What you think, you become."
Buddha

The first element of success is developing a mindset that can support your transformation. At least half of your energy should be focused on how to change your current thinking process and create a "can do" attitude.

Until you modify how you think, your behavior will likely never change due to long-held habits. Familiarity offers a certain sense of stability and comfort, especially when processing information quickly. But familiar and outdated habits are the quicksand that sticks you in an obsolete status quo which must change in order to allow you to grow.

There are two key elements in changing your mindset:

- The first is to believe that you can make a change.
- The second is to fully embrace the fact that change means dealing with the unknown.

As humans, our brains have been "hardwired" to fear the unfamiliar. This survival instinct protects us (and keeps us safe) in dangerous situations.

Being uncomfortable with change is human and predictable. But the key is to recognize that fear is part of the process. It can also be a paralyzing force that keeps you stuck in the proverbial mud.

You can change what you eat, how you move your body and how you see your future when you program your mind to accept your new reality. It is not easy. But it can be done and could be your ticket to health.

Below are eight questions that should help you shift your mindset and create a new reality that supports your objectives of conquering obesity and lead to a healthier, more enjoyable life.

Your goal is to find two or three key answers to each question. Take your time. Be honest with yourself. This is for you only. They will help you develop a picture of what you need to do in order to develop a meaningful plan for lasting change.

- What really matters to me in life?
- How are my current activities supporting what I really want to accomplish?
- What has prevented me from making necessary changes to reach my objectives?
- How can I best identify what I need to change; and why is this change important to me?
- What changes will be easy for me to make by myself?
- Which of my desired changes will require help from others?
- What is the most difficult change I must make, and why?
- What must I do differently in order to start believing in myself and in my ability to reach my desired future?

When you invest the time to address these, a realistic picture begins to emerge. It reveals how to identify the barriers that prevent you from being successful in your quest for a healthier and more productive life.

Use Questions to Change your Mindset.

Relying on questions to modify your mindset is the fundamental principle of Dr. Marilee Adams' work on the methodology she calls "Question Thinking." Dr. Adams shows how the questions we ask ourselves—and the questions we pose to the world around us—have a profound effect on our behavior and the choices we make, in her words, "moment, by moment, by moment."

The model she has developed is simple, yet quite powerful. As Dr. Adams explains, *"the questions you ask yourself or of others, lead to decisions which produce action, and results. It is important to reflect on these results. And when they are not what you want, examining the actions or the decisions is not enough. You have to review the questions you ask yourself."*

It's like taking an examination in school. We grow more by learning what we *don't know,* than from taking easy tests that measure nothing. The harder, and more honest, the questions we ask ourselves, the more we learn. This is how you can start changing your mindset.

Given the way our brains work, and the way we are hard-wired for survival, the questions we naturally ask are those that protect us and that focus on what went wrong, who's to blame, and what is the problem with ourselves and others. We cannot ignore them, and must recognize and accept this natural "avoidance" tendency as part of our human nature.

However, there is another way to respond and view the world, a more positive approach that draws on our curiosity and the realm of possibilities. When we learn to slow down the natural tendency to go into a protective mode of blame and fear, and start to ask questions such as, *"What are the real facts here? What went right in the situation? How well did I use my skills here? What can I learn from this?"* we can then start to create shifts in our thinking process and experience more positive outcomes in our day-to-day lives.

As you choose to make changes in your life, paying attention to your questions and corresponding thought processes can make a big—and very positive—difference.

As you continue to learn about others' journeys into a healthier lifestyle, it becomes clear that a shift in mindset is a key element to long-term success.

Kay's Story: A Shift to a Mindset of Embracing Change.

The shift of her mindset was a key element for Kay's success, along with her ability to stay true to her decision to regain her health by adopting a regular exercise program and re-learning to make healthier food choices. Sharing her experience, Kay offered the following insights:

> *"After the jolt of the news from the doctor* [about the seriousness of her health condition, aggravated by the obesity] *my mindset shifted into survival mode, because it became clear that if I wanted to continue living, I had to do something about my weight. I decided that I did want to live and be happy with my life. It was the survivor in me that finally won out over my sedentary sloth.*
>
> *That's when I started taking real action. I began to embrace my daily walks, even welcomed the pain and discomfort because it made me feel that I was actually accomplishing something. My confidence—and the positive physical results of my new activity—became easier*

to see.

This led to more—and better—changes. I stopped buying fast food and started watching what I ate. I knew how to eat healthy; I just hadn't done it up until then. I admit to an occasional relapse. But I caught myself quickly, reaccepted my new mindset as an ongoing process of constant improvement, and soldiered on by using my freedom to say: 'No, I don't want that. It's a waste of money and my spirit.'

My Story: The Compelling Reason that Shifted My Mindset

Losing weight was not a new goal in my life. I tried most of the known diets and had a measure of success in shedding pounds—for a time. But the weight always came back. I fully understood—intellectually—that I needed to change habits and priorities if I wanted to reach a healthier weight. However, I could lead an active life, had a successful family life and career, and believed I was doing well, in spite of being obese. But as I got older, my ability to carry the extra pounds that I could when I was younger became more difficult.

As explained by Dr. Kane, this is not an uncommon issue for the obese:

"From a medical perspective, there are many health conditions associated with obesity. These include diabetes, high blood pressure, coronary artery disease, cancer, obstructive sleep apnea, cardiomyopathies, arthritic issues, infertility, menstrual irregularities, COPD, (chronic obstructive pulmonary disease), or obesity-induced asthma.

> *The obese typically suffer at least one of these additional afflictions. But it's easier for the young to live with obesity. And yet, as the obese age, one or more of the above conditions work in unison to make their lifestyle more difficult to endure. Young people, who may be obese, assuming they are fit and active, may not have any discernible medical problems outside of minor sleep apnea and maybe some mild arthritic issues. But, eventually, problems such as high blood pressure and cholesterol levels, or some form of glucose intolerance, will inevitability begin to affect the health of an aging obese person, and not for the better."*

So, knowing the potential problems that were "out there waiting for me," was not sufficient. Something had yet to click in my head to create the necessary motivation to act on what I knew was waiting—somewhere around the corner—for me!!

Then, the bell went off in my head at, of all places, the middle of the Philadelphia airport!

In 2008, I was still travelling for business about 60 percent of my time and at my highest weight (over 300 pounds on a 5' 8" body). I had torn the meniscus on my right knee and had an operation to repair what the surgeon called "a serious tear." I needed a cane to help me walk. This is NOT fun for one who must travel almost every week!

Arriving on a flight, late, and at the gate near the far end of the terminal—a considerable trek to begin with—I was struggling to make it to the baggage claim area. I was tired, angry, and my knee was painful. There was no cart available to help me, I was too proud to ask for a wheel chair, but not too proud to feel sorry for my fat self.

And then it hit me from out of the blue, as strongly as if I had been Saul on the road to Damascus. If I didn't do something different, and take better care of my health, I would not see my newborn granddaughter graduate from college. And I so badly wanted to do that.

There was my compelling reason, staring straight at me as I leaned on that cane in the middle of the Philly airport. It was a true epiphany. And though it was caused by external, irritating events, my deep desire to fundamentally change finally arrived. This was my "burning platform" and I knew, without any doubt, that I had to get off it!

In talking with so many people who have lost and kept their weight off, this is one of **the** most important elements for success: Make the change for YOURSELF, for something that is important to YOU, not to please others, or to yield to outside pressures. And—fresh from that profound experience—I finished my long trek to baggage claim, finally filled with a true resolve to begin my journey to a healthy weight and a more fulfilling new life.

Choosing the Right Meals for Your Needs

"Your body needs the proper fuel to be the home for your soul. Take care of your body, and it will take care of you."
Tiza Pyle

If you have selected WLS as the way to reach your ideal weight, the surgery will require you to make significant modifications in your eating habits and the types of food you eat.

Depending on the type of surgery you've had, the way you absorb the nutrients in food has been altered and you may need to correct this deficiency with vitamins and other supplements as recommended by your doctor. However, the most important change after any type of WLS is becoming aware of the amount of food your new stomach will tolerate, and making the necessary changes in your habits to support your ability to maintain your healthy weight for life.

As evident by the many diet theories—all claiming to be *the definitive solution* for the obesity issue—there is a lot of confusion about what to do. I believe there is no ONE ideal diet for losing and keeping off extra weight. **You should find the approach that is right for you and your body, based on key principles of nutrition and your doctor's recommendations.** And since you will be limited to eating only small amounts of food after your WLS, you must make sure you are eating foods that pack the most nutritional value.

When reviewing the many dietary theories available,

one constant is obvious: to lose weight you must eat less food. And there is no magic formula that will make you shed the unwanted pounds—even when the headlines in magazines promise incredible results! However, many of these theories have consistent themes that are summarized below. These "healthy nutrition" principles make sense and should govern your approach:

- Eat whole fresh foods, rather than the packaged "processed" variety that many are accustomed to. Another reason to avoid processed foods is their high levels of chemical additives and fillers.
- Eat lean meats and fish; these provide vital protein you need after WLS.
- Incorporate fat in your diet—fat is not the enemy. Fats are needed for healthy cell development and nutrition. There is much information on the "healthy fats" that need to be part of your daily nutritional choices.
- Increase the number of green raw vegetables. Dark green vegetables have higher nutritional value.
- Eat fresh fruits, with a low glycemic index, such as dark red fruits which contain high antioxidant levels.
- Limit—or avoid, if you can—sugar and salt.
- Limit your carbohydrate intake, especially foods made with processed grains (such as bleached flour and white rice).
- Avoid drinks with high sugar content (processed fruit juices, carbonated beverages, etc.) and limit your consumption of alcoholic beverages.
- Drink water to keep your body hydrated.
- Whenever possible eat fresh, locally grown food.

After the surgery, your body will respond differently to some foods. Certainly, the amount you eat is a significant difference that must be addressed. Also, given the changes in your digestive system, certain foods can make you sick: such as fats, sugars and carbohydrates, as they move faster though your—now smaller—digestive tract. A smaller digestive area means some foods are not efficiently processed, in most cases, sugars and carbohydrates. You must modify your food intake habits to accommodate this. Below are three simple ideas to help you develop new, healthier habits around food. And though these are straightforward, they require commitment to change old habits that probably have been part of your life for many years.

Learn to listen to your body. This is a new feeling for many obese people. Start by making sure you know when you've had enough to eat. Then stop so your body isn't compelled to throw up the extra food. Throwing up can happen after WLS surgery until you learn to recognize the warning signs that you've had enough!

Commit to chewing your food. Most obese people don't take the time to chew their food properly. Digestion starts in the mouth. Your smaller stomach will thank your teeth for helping it along. You can start doing this before surgery—like today!

Slow down your eating. Eating food—good food—should be pleasurable, not a task. If you teach yourself to eat leisurely, and savor the wonderful food you are enjoying, you'll eat less, chew well, and discover how delightful your meals—and the new foods that are now a part of your life—can be.

Other Acquired "Good Food" Behaviors after WLS

After the surgery, you need to concentrate on eating enough protein to sustain healthy muscle mass. This is very important because protein helps to build good muscle, replacing all the fat you are losing.

Within the initial months after surgery, the amount of food you can consume at any one time will be small, and you may feel hungry during the day. Be prepared to have some food prepared for "between-meal snacks" such as a piece of fruit, some raw vegetables, a small baked potato, etc. (not a donut!!). This is a good habit to get into after your surgery.

After about a year, you will grow comfortable eating the ounces of protein you need in each meal, a half-cup of a cooked vegetable, and a small salad. With the adequate amount of protein, you will not feel hungry. Large meals are a part of your past! Embrace your new life of small portions that satisfy you, and help maintain your healthy weight.

Learning How to Eat Well in a Restaurant

Portions offered at American restaurants are super-sized and much more than anybody needs to eat under almost any circumstance. You will become more aware of this as your post-surgery eating habits change. You will also quickly learn new behaviors that better support your individual needs. Below are a few new things to try when eating out:

Have fun exploring the appetizer menu. This is probably all you might be able to eat anyway. So look for high protein appetizers, or ask for them (salmon, steak, chicken). Combine with a small salad and you have your main meal.

Ask servers if they have half-portion entrees. One favorite for a Sunday brunch is a half-order of eggs Benedict. And if you don't eat the bread, you have a healthier option for a protein-rich meal (and more room in your smaller stomach).

Share meals with those at your table. This is an easy way to lower the cost of going out, satisfy your need, and help a spouse or friend eat smaller portions.

Ask for substitutions. Learn to ask for what you want, that also meets your new food needs. Most restaurants are more than happy to accommodate special menu requests. And if they don't, consider finding a place that will! For instance, most restaurants will give you an additional serving of vegetables instead of the potatoes. It is healthier, less filling, and you will avoid those higher amounts of carbohydrates.

Avoid the bread before the meal. This habit can prevent you from being able to eat what you order. Your small stomach will already be full when the main course arrives. You may even want to avoid the temptation by asking the server to remove the breadbasket from your table to be safer! But check with others at your table!

As part of your preparation for surgery, you were probably required to be on a medically supervised diet. This is an important aspect of the program, as you learn about food choices, types of food to eat and avoid, different diet theories, etc. All this knowledge is very helpful in learning how to make the right food choices after your surgery.

Preparing yourself for this change is very important, as your relationship with food will be different after surgery.

Much of this information is incorporated in the preparation phase of WLS surgery. But, if the clinic you select for your procedure does not do this, remember that there are many good sources of nutrition information. And like most people who have dealt with obesity, you may already have a wealth of knowledge from your earlier attempts to lose weight. WLS is a powerful new tool. And you can easily incorporate what you already know into an effective plan for healthier living.

By learning how to properly eat after the surgery, you are protecting your emotional investment. Your new body will experience changes that require commitment and energy to create the success you want—a healthier you!

Final Thoughts on Food, Meals, and Better Post-WLS Health

In addition to eating the proper—and ideal amounts—of food after your WLS, you will need to take a multiple vitamin and some supplements as recommended by your physician for the rest of your life. Since WLS changes how—and how efficiently—your system absorbs food, you are likely to have normal vitamin deficiencies, especially B12, an essential vitamin for good health.

You must also commit to regular, annual check-ups with your physician. Blood tests can be done to ensure the levels of essential vitamins in your system are correct and that you are taking the appropriate amounts of necessary supplements to sustain your optimal health and longevity. This is important!

Making Movement a Part of Your Life

"Learn to move your body and have fun.
Create a new way of thinking and challenge yourself to a healthier and more enjoyable way of being."
Tiza Pyle

The third ***M*** of the ***Holistic Circle of Health—*** movement—is perhaps the hardest to maintain. Exercise alone does not help with weight loss. So why is this such an important step?

Most obese people are not used to normal mobility or any type of physical activity. This is easy to grasp since both were probably painful. However, as you begin losing weight and regain health, one of the most important changes you must consider is to making regular exercise part of a daily routine. You must learn—or re-learn—how to move your body in ways that are sustainable, fun, and can be done regularly for the rest of your life.

Our model uses the word "movement" as a key element of success. You don't need to go to a gym. But you need to regularly move your body in order to keep your energy, build muscle mass, and flexibility to ensure a richer life experience as you age.

Renewed vigor is another benefit to maintaining a healthy weight. Age is no excuse. Through exercise you find strength and motivation to continue doing what want you to do. Simply-put, regular exercise is in itself, self-fulfilling.

Muscle burns calories much more efficiently than fat. As you create a more healthy balance between fat and muscle, it's easier to maintain your healthy weight.

Exercise is also an effective way to relieve stress and even reverse the effects of depression. Regular exercise creates endorphins in your brain that support vigorous lifestyles and promote mental health.

Following are some suggestions of what I have used in order to incorporate more movement into my daily routine. There are many ways to keep your body strong and fit, but you need to find activities that are safe for you, and meet your individual needs and health condition. Below are descriptions of activities that have worked well for me, and are **not** recommendations of exercises that might work for all. **It is essential to check with your health care provider before starting any type of exercise routine.**

- **Walking**. Research reveals that daily walks are the best type of exercise for any age. There are many large indoor places to walk, even in the cold months of the year (shopping malls, for example). I have a "buddy" to make these walks more fun.
- **Dancing.** Ballroom dancing and square dance groups can be a lot of fun. Both are great ways to aerobically exercise, not to mention make new friends.
- **Gardening**. Being outdoors, weeding flowerbeds, and other gardening-related activities can help you become more agile and promote physical stamina. And who doesn't want to be outdoors in nice weather and have some quiet time for yourself?
- **Training your dog**. A training class with your dog can offer lots of fun and exercise for you and the dog. It also offers the opportunity to meet others with similar interests. The daily walks can be a

healthy benefit with "man's best friend" as a loyal companion.

- **Volunteer Activities**. Find some enjoyable activity that helps you move. For example, working with small children. The little ones will keep you active, and helping in daycare centers can also be spiritually fulfilling as you provide a valuable service.

For some, joining a gym is the best idea. You may consider some options available in your neighborhood and build an enjoyable exercise routine that fits your lifestyle. There is a great deal of positive energy when you are physically active with others who have similar interests and think the same way as you. Some exercise machines available in a gym are a great way to keep track of your progress. And, when your physician approves, you can try other types of exercise programs such as Yoga, Pilates, Zumba, or Kickboxing, to name a few. Look for a community of people who can support you in your journey.

When you make exercise a foundation of your healthy lifestyle, the benefits are all positive and you'll become quickly surprised at how much better you feel. Be creative! Find something you like to do, something that is easy to begin and grow with, as you push your "personal envelope" a little more each day.

However, make sure to consult your physician before making any changes in your daily level of activity.

Karen's Story: Making Exercise an Integral Part of Her Life

Karen's experience after WLS highlights how she was able to make exercise an essential part of her transformation process.

After surgically losing more than 200 pounds, she underwent plastic surgery due to significant issues with extra skin. So her challenges not only included a healthier lifestyle, but better skin and muscle tone.

Talking about her experience with exercise after surgery, Karen shares these insights:

> *"Knowing the importance of exercise, I bought an elliptical bike when I was heavier. I was so excited. But after reading the pamphlet, I learned that the maximum weight it could support was 225 pounds. And I weighed 350 at the time. It was disappointing that I couldn't use it. But as soon as I hit 225 after surgery, I hopped on that bike that cost me $700 and was ready to get my money's worth!*
>
> *At first, I was barely able to stay on it for more than a few minutes. But by working at it every day, I consistently built up my endurance! By the time I started getting bored with it, I was up to an hour—a* **vigorous** *hour.*
>
> *I was ready for a real bicycle: to 'get up and* **go somewhere**!*' I rode that thing the whole summer and had a blast! Then a girlfriend invited me to her Zumba class. And that's where my opinion of 'real exercise' turned around. Before that it was a chore. But exhaustive exercise—like Zumba—was so much fun. I felt like I was dancing with my girlfriends and Zumba classes became a three-times-a-week ritual.*

Then I added weight training through one of my Zumba instructors who doubled as a personal trainer. And through that—and Zumba—I hit my goal of 175 pounds. What a sweet victory!

After I reached my desired weight, I then had plastic surgery to remove the large amount of loose skin due to all that lost weight. It was a medical necessity to avoid skin rashes and other uncomfortable situations. This was also quite successful and I feel like another person. I now have the body of a much younger, healthier woman. Recently somebody asked me if I was 29! Actually, I'm closer to 50 than 30 years old!"

Karen explains how she prepared herself for this second surgery to remove all that excess skin after her weight loss. She shares the meal plan that works well for her.

"Working with my trainer, I was determined to go into those surgeries in the best physical shape I could muster. I worked hard for months! This really paid off. These are long surgical procedures which can take eight to 10 hours. So being in top physical shape really helped. In the hospital, the nurses roused me out of bed and walked me down the hallway a few hours after the surgery. I was able to get right up and walk with little trouble. Many were astounded and attributed this to the fact I was in such good shape.

My surgeon also complimented my ability to heal much better than all her other patients. I owe it to my Zumba and two weight training sessions per week, not to mention jogging or running 10 miles, three times each week prior to my skin removal surgeries."

As part of her preparation for surgery, Karen also describes the diet she followed to be in the best shape for the procedures. She calls it her "super clean" eating program and still incorporates much of it to this day.

Breakfast: Gluten free oats with a couple of dried apricots and some flax meal and almond milk.

Lunch: 3 to 5 oz. of lean protein such as chicken breast or turkey, some steamed vegetables, usually broccoli or other dark green vegetable, and brown rice or a sweet potato.

Dinner: Mostly protein, usually meat and brown rice or a sweet potato.

Between Meals: Plenty of fresh water and no snacking. Sodas and other carbonated drinks are **Verboten** *because they give me too much gas. Water and iced tea are my best alternatives. If I* **must** *eat between meals, a rice cake is a good option to kill those hunger pangs.*

Limited amount of coffee, with some milk and artificial sweetener, if I must!

What Karen describes may be pretty close to an ideal eating program for long-term weight maintenance after WLS. It is strict, but can deliver results and—if your physician approves—may be a program you can adopt for a period of time if you see some weight gain after WLS.

Most people find that maintaining weight is much harder than losing it. This is why you need to be careful and have a good plan.

Karen also shared interesting insights about food, addiction, and ways to redirect our energy to avoid using food as a mechanism to reduce stress or replace other needs:

> *"I believe that overeating is a form of addiction. You must find a different outlet. Many people habitually jump from one addiction to another because they have addictive personalities: alcoholics, shopaholics; foodaholics. Many feel compelled to find something more productive. Though I don't view myself as the addictive type, I replaced food with exercise.*
>
> *After my bariatric surgery I became emotionally overwhelmed. Eventually, when confronted with situations where I normally would turn to food to help me through, I started exercising. Now, exercise is a better solution—rather than inhaling a big bowl of ice cream—to deal with my problems and frustration."*

Karen has taken control of her life in many ways. She's added exercise to her daily routine to keep herself active, controls her emotions, and tones her body. Because of the great amount of weight she has lost, Karen used plastic surgery to redefine her smaller, fitter body. She eventually became a Zumba instructor. Karen had discovered an easy and fun way to ensure she stays active and committed to a vigorous lifestyle that supports her goal of a healthy weight—for life.

Defining Success

"You are the owner of your life and the architect of your future. Learn to live on your own terms and know real success."
Tiza Pyle

Much has been written about success, and how to define it. Defining success is not the objective of this chapter. What you will learn here is how to define **your** version of success.

If you have been obese for many years, doing simple activities is probably difficult. So make a list of what you can do now and what you were not able to do before the surgery and weight loss. This alone will give you a reference point to measure your success. Sometimes being able to walk without pain, play with your children or grandchildren, climb stairs without being out of breath, or take less medication are all great gifts to measure your success.

Developing your own internal mechanism to measure victories and accomplishments becomes very important, especially as the years go by. Many of your current friends and colleagues may never have seen you in the days you were dealing with obesity. At the start of your weight loss process, you received much encouragement from those who saw the changes in your body and your behavior. However, over time, some may see you and think you still need to be thinner! Also, friends may forget how you used to look and feel. You cannot rely on outside encouragement to stay the course. You must develop your own definition of success and be able to celebrate your new life.

The following three elements can help you reach your success objectives:

Establishing Accountability. When you are truly accountable, you take responsibility for your choices and your life. You don't make excuses. You ***do***! When deciding on what works best for you, remember that accountability is something only you can do, but you don't have to do it alone.

- Ask for help! Get others involved in your journey.
- Make it fun. Find activities, methods and processes that make sense for you, your personality, and lifestyle. Incorporate them into your plan to stay the course for life.
- Learn from your mistakes, and correct them. Accept that the road will have bumps, but you can overcome them. Everyone makes mistakes. But you don't have to repeat them.
- Take charge of your life and build the future you want.

Developing Meaningful Metrics. There are many ways to measure success in your journey to reach a healthy weight for life. Using scales tends to be a universally accepted method, in spite of the pitfalls. Body weight fluctuates widely. And as you may well know, people tend to become so fixated in achieving a "magic number," that other more meaningful measurements are missed. Here are some suggestions of other ways you can gauge your progress after surgery; **your physician can help you in this process.**

- If you take medication for various health conditions, measure your progress as you move toward healthier levels of blood pressure, cholesterol and triglycerides, to ideally reduce dosages or even eliminate the need for these medications—**but only with your physician's approval and direction!**

- Record your level of physical activity, such as how many blocks you can walk, how well you can climb stairs, or stay active without an extended rest. You will be surprised with your progress as you move closer to your desired healthier weight. Physical activity is a key element of your long-term success.
- Make some "change in your eating habits" goals and track them. For example: I tracked how many times I ate dark green vegetables, what foods I chose to eliminate from my daily diet, my successes (and where I fell short). Maybe you want to record how many times you experiment with new foods and how those went. Even in today's world of computers and data recording, inexpensive spiral notebooks are a really fun way to track your post-operative/on the way to a "new you" story. Make a game of it, and have fun.

By creating your own new "measuring stick" for yourself, it's easier to see your progress on your terms and celebrate success in reaching your healthier lifestyle.

Tracking your progress. In the corporate world there is an old management adage that says that you can't manage what you don't measure. Some argue that all the really important things in life cannot be measured and there's some truth to that, too. However, unless you measure something, you don't know if it is getting better or worse. You can only manage for improvement once you develop a clear idea of what is improving and what isn't. This is true for tracking your progress of improving your health and reaching your goal for a weight that supports your objective. It is important that you think about what will be easier. Today there are many tools that can help you do this. Here is a list of ideas that may help you track your progress:

- Use the scale as a tool to measure progress. But as already suggested, don't obsess on what it tells you. Weighing yourself weekly—rather than daily—might be a good way to place the scale in perspective. Choose one a day a week to take this regular measurement. If you can use Microsoft Excel or other computer tools, it's easier to calculate your progress, create charts and calculate percentage of body weight lost, etc. If not, that spiral notebook we spoke of and a calculator work just as well. Your doctor can give you tips on calculating and should also be able to provide you with BMI charts to reference. Or, of course, you can find them on the web.
- Use a pedometer to calculate the number of steps you take each day. There are many good, affordable ones to choose from that can give you a fine understanding of your daily activity level. Record your results and set daily—or weekly—goals for your activity that are attainable.
- Working with your physician, determine two or three factors to measure improvement such as blood pressure, cholesterol and triglyceride levels, body mass index (BMI) and any other pertinent measurement that applies to your own health

situation. These indicators can be checked periodically by your doctor and will become accurate benchmarks of your progress toward being healthier and less dependent on medication.

As you continue to change old habits and start new ones, tracking your progress in any way that makes sense to you is worth the effort. It can provide you with a clear indication of where you have been and where you are now. Measurements also help when you need to go back and remember your journey, especially on days when it is hard to stay the course!

5 Lessons I Have Learned from Being Fat

"I have been fat and I have been thin
... thin is better."
YOU!

These five lessons are a good summary of my journey to better health. My only objective in sharing my experience and story is to offer sound ideas to support you in your journey to a healthier, productive and exciting new life.

1. What you think and believe about yourself has a lot to do with how you respond to life.

All my life I had to deal with the belief that I was fat, when the reality was that I was tall, muscular and very athletic. I was not the ideal "type" in a culture where being petite, less active and more "feminine" was the preferred norm. Being the opposite led me to becoming fat. When you believe you are fat, and don't fit in well, your behavior begins to reflect this "truth." Eventually, I ended up gaining enough weight to become morbidly obese—which turned out to be a self-fulfilling prophecy, from my earlier beliefs.

So my lesson here is that you must be prepared to examine and challenge the thoughts and beliefs that you carry in order to create the opportunity for a new reality for your life.

2. Being overweight, or even obese, does not prevent you from being successful.

I am a good example of this. I have a successful career,

a great marriage, friends, community involvement, and even more blessings. Being fat did not stop me from those successes. I was going to "make it" and show people that I was not going to be defined by my weight, and being fat was not the "real me."

But therein lies the problem of not taking care of your body and your health. You can create a protective barrier that justifies your unhealthy behaviors and how you see the issue of being overweight. The price I paid for this was my health, especially as I got older.

3. Find one significant "compelling reason" to sustain your resolve to change. This is the key to success.

Change is not easy. It requires creating new patterns of behavior and eliminating habits that are engrained in our brains. Habits develop over time and become part of who we are. Letting go of old habits and replacing them with new ones is hard work and demands focus and persistence. This is one of the main reasons why so many who try to change habits in order to lose weight are unsuccessful.

In order to stay the course and do the work to develop new habits and behaviors, you need a reason that is meaningful to YOU. Some organizations call it the "burning platform"—that single compelling inspiration that gives you no other option but to change. It becomes an irresistible force. The pain of NOT changing has to be greater than the pain of making the change.

4. Take time to discover and accept what is right for YOU.

Social pressures about weight are enormous. Not everybody has the same body type, or follows the same approach to eating, or defines "ideal weight" based on a chart. You must be inquisitive and find out what is right for YOU. It took me some time to get there. But eventually, I accepted who I was, and made the best of it. My current weight is the HEALTHY one for me, not what is on a chart. And that's all that counts.

The lesson is this: Being healthy is about creating more meaningful metrics that are associated with health, not looks, or a number on a scale. Your healthcare provider can help you create these personal goals that make the best sense for you.

5. Final Lesson: Believe in yourself and your ability to take the path that is right for you.

For many years, being fat was associated with lack of will power, laziness, and low self-esteem. Only recently has obesity been viewed as a true medical problem, with causes reaching far beyond the "lack of will-power or self-control," that was commonly accepted. However, the social stigma is still strong and cannot be ignored. What allowed me to achieve a healthy weight was my acceptance of the fact that I was doing this for me, instead of "caving in" to social pressure. By being a more normal size today, I admit to having opportunities that were unavailable to me before, though I cannot be completely certain. That's because I believe opportunities usually come to us only when we're ready to embrace them.

And yet, it's clear to me that only when I made the mental shift—changed my mindset—about how I see food and activity, was I able to change the past behaviors that had kept me from achieving long-term success. My new approach has allowed me to reach a healthy weight and to have developed a plan that will allow me to maintain my goal for the rest of my life.

This is what I wish for each of you who embark on this journey of maintaining a body weight that is right for YOU, that helps you be healthy, and live the life you want to.

Making it Happen: Staying the Course for the Long Haul

"One essential element of success is focus and continuity. Make a commitment to yourself to embark in this journey of health."
Tiza Pyle

You are beginning a lifelong journey. And it is natural to sometimes feel like giving up when it seems so hard. And as the years go by, you may regain some of the weight lost after your surgery. Don't worry, it's normal. It doesn't mean you are a failure, or that all is lost. This "all or nothing" thinking can be damaging. Remember to stay positive and focus on your goals—day-by-day—for the long haul.

When you feel like giving up, remain strong and reaffirm your goals. You'll feel a great sense of pride, confidence and accomplishment when you overcome these temporary times and don't give in to all the easy distractions that conspire against you. Staying true to your goals makes you stronger, builds confidence, improves your health, and makes you feel unstoppable.

As discussed earlier, find a support structure than can be of assistance to you during harder times. One of my favorite sayings about staying motivated is that, "*only you can motivate yourself, but you do not need to do it alone*!" Learn to ask for help! There is a large and strong community that understands your struggles and is ready to lend a hand.

In the past few years I have learned a lot about personal changes, including adjusting to retirement, moving to a new city, starting my business, losing over 100 pounds, developing new eating habits, starting a regular exercise program, and I can go on.

I had to change many things about my activities—and myself—in order to adjust and to create new meaning and purpose for my life. What I learned can help you be successful in your own change process, and stay the course you have chosen.

10 Golden Rules for Personal Change: How to Develop New Habits for Success

1. Select only one thing to focus on at any given time and be committed to that course of action.
2. Develop a written plan of what you want to accomplish and how you are going to do it.
3. Develop a support network.
4. Know what motivates you.
5. Think about possible obstacles and how to overcome them.
6. Develop an easy method to measure progress.
7. Create a way to be accountable to others (and to yourself).
8. Know the triggers that can derail your motivation.
9. Keep your focus on the desired results/outcome.
10. Be prepared to "stay the course for the long run" and embrace failures as learning opportunities.

You can find more detailed information on each one of the items listed above in my article that you can download from:

YourPathToSuccessCoaching.com/bookresources

The password to access these resources is:

FATHURTS2016

Section IV
Resources

Tools and Guides for Long Term Success

Any printed material has limited life, and a way to make the material fresh and updated is to use on-line resources.

I have been successful using a variety of tools to help clarify my thinking, get focused, and develop greater self-awareness for successful changes. The tools offered as resources here are intended as additional support you can use in your journey of transformation. They have been designed to provide you with a compass to navigate the sea of change, help you record important thoughts and ideas, and to be accountable for your progress.

All tools and templates can be found at:
YourPathToSuccessCoaching.com/bookresources
The password to access these resources is:
FATHURTS2016

You are invited to visit the site and download all the forms you believe can be of value to you. The site will be updated regularly, so plan to check there to see if new tools and templates have been added.

In addition, you will find some suggested websites you can access to get further information on the topics discussed in the book. You can search for information on bariatric surgery, nutrition and other related topics on the sites listed. There are many others, but these were the ones I have used, and found helpful.

Bibliography and Recommended Books

Below is a list of books that I have read and helped me formulate some of the concepts and models I offer in this book. There are many other good books on bariatric surgery, nutrition theories, change management and behavior changes. The various citations in the text of the book come from the resources listed below.

If you have an interest in getting more information in any of these books, a quick search on Amazon.com will provide you with a wealth of information.

Change Your Questions, Change Your Life: 10 Powerful Tools for Life and Work by Marilee Adams (June 1, 2009)

Transitions: Making Sense of Life's Changes by William Bridges (Aug 11, 2004)

The Structure of Scientific Revolutions, 3rd Edition by Thomas S. Kuhn (Dec. 15, 1996)

Your Brain at Work: Strategies for Overcoming Distraction, Regaining Focus, and Working Smarter All Day Long by David Rock (Oct 6, 2009)

Just Enough: Tools for Creating Success in Your Work and Life by Laura Nash and Howard Stevenson (March 10, 2005)

Epi-paleo Rx: The Prescription for Disease

Reversal and Optimal Health by Dr. Jack Kruse (Feb 20, 2013)

Grain Brain: The Surprising Truth about Wheat, Carbs, and Sugar—Your Brain's Silent Killers by David Perlmutter (Jan 16, 2014)

Sugar Blues by William Dufty (Mar 17, 1986)

The Weight Loss Surgery Workbook: Deciding on Bariatric Surgery, Preparing for the Procedure, and Changing Habits for Post-Surgery Success by Doreen A. Samelson and Arnold D. Salzberg (May 1, 2011)

The Blood Sugar Solution: The Ultra-Healthy Program for Losing Weight, Preventing Disease, and Feeling Great Now! By Mark Hyman (Feb 28, 2012)

Why We Get Fat: And What to Do About It by Gary Taubes (Dec 27, 2011)

The Big Fat Surprise: Why Butter, Meat and Cheese Belong in a Healthy Diet by Nina Teicholz (May 13, 2014)

SuperFoods Smoothies: 100 Delicious, Energizing & Nutrient-dense Recipes by Julie Morris (May 7, 2013)

About the Author

Dr. Beatriz ("Tiza") M. Pyle, (PhD) brings to her coaching practice expertise and knowledge in change processes, executive coaching and leadership development. Her experience and commitment to guide each client to achieve results and reach their goals are powerful tools for personal transformation.

Many of her clients, recognizing that good health is a key factor in performing at one's best, have started looking for different approaches to leadership development—those that include a more balanced outlook to their lives, including health and nutrition goals. This has reinforced Tiza's own belief in the importance of wellness in ones' life; and it supported by her own experience. She was able to regain her health and energy in her 60's by tackling her own obesity problem and developing an exciting, more active lifestyle after significant weight loss.

Tiza's current work is rooted in the belief that "an active longevity" is a reachable goal. And she is committed to support her clients in developing a doable plan for a productive, long life.

Having competed a year-long training program in nutrition and wellness coaching at the Institute for Integrative Nutrition (IIN) in 2013, Tiza offers her clients an opportunity to work on a holistic approach to life—Mindset, Movement and Meals (The 3 Ms)—as an integral part of their individual transformation.

Tiza's formal education includes:

- PhD in Education from Loyola University of Chicago
- Master's degree in Human Resources Management from Loyola University of Chicago
- BS degree in Education at the Universidade Federal de Minas Gerais, Brazil
- Graduate from the Institute for Integrative Nutrition (IIN) as a Health Coach

Tiza is the Founder and CEO of Pyle Consulting Group, Inc. and offers coaching programs as *Your Path to Success Coaching*, a division of Pyle Consulting Group, Inc. She and her husband live in St. Charles, Illinois, USA.

How to Engage with Tiza

My principal reason for writing this book is to share with others who want to make changes in their lives, what I have learned on my own journey of transformation.

I welcome your comments, suggestions and ideas on the topics of personal transformation and change, health and wellness and your experience with weight-loss surgery. We can learn from each other, and support our quest for a rewarding new reality.

Coaching is a great way to accelerate your progress, and achieve your goals, and we offer a variety of options to our clients. We have both individual and group programs.

Visit our website
www.YourPathToSuccessCoaching.com

You can leave messages and make comments on the site. Use the ***Contact Us*** area to communicate with me.

You can also reach me via e-mail, and on social media on LinkedIn and Facebook.

E-mail: Tiza@YourPathtoSuccessCoaching.com
Facebook page: YourPathtoSuccessCoaching
LinkedIn: https://www.linkedin.com/in/tizapyle

I look forward to hearing from you.

Tiza